A PRIMER IN PHENOMENOLOGICAL PSYCHOLOGY

Ernest Keen

Bucknell University

UNIVERSITY
PRESS OF
AMERICA

LANHAM • NEW YORK • LONDON

For Deej and Christa

Copyright © 1975 by
Holt, Rinehart and Winston, Inc.

University Press of America,® Inc.

4720 Boston Way
Lanham, MD 20706

3 Henrietta Street
London WC2E 8LU England

Printed in the United States of America

Reprinted by arrangement with CBS College Publishing

Library of Congress Cataloging in Publication Data

Keen, Ernest, 1937-

A primer in phenomenological psychology.

Originally published: New York : Holt, Rinehart,
and Winston, 1975.
Includes index.
1. Phenomenological psychology. I. Title.
BF204.5.K43   1982   150.19'2   81-40901
ISBN 0-8191-2262-9 (pbk.)   AACR2

PREFACE

There are many ways to do psychology. This book describes doing psychology phenomenologically. It is intended for the beginning student, but I hope that colleagues who want to learn about phenomenological psychology will also find the book helpful. Doing psychology phenomenologically is, strangely, extremely easy and incredibly difficult at the same time. It is easy because we are all native phenomenologists; we all have experiences, reflect upon them, and interpret them, and in doing so we live our lives more or less successfully. We usually fail to notice the tremendous amount of experiential understanding involved in simply living; a fish is the last one to discover water. Our understanding is already implicitly there, ready to be appreciated, articulated, and developed into psychological sophistication.

The difficulties of phenomenological psychology arise from the complexities that emerge when we take the investigation of experience seriously. Perhaps psychologists (at least in the United States) have not yet developed phenomenological psychology very vigorously because we know how complex the texture and structure of human experience really are. If it is true that fools rush in where angels fear to tread, we may be foolish to try it now. We are committing ourselves to what may seem an impossible task: to explore human experience as it is lived every day.

A number of American psychologists have made notable attacks on the issue of everyday subjective experience. For those well acquainted with psychology, I have included a postscript on the place of phenomenology in American psychology, explaining how the approach in this book relates to more familiar attempts to write a psychology of experience. This book thus offers *a* phenomenological psychology, instead of *the* phenomenological approach in psychology.

There are four parts to this primer. In Part I we leap right in. By exploring a single episode of less than an hour's duration (Chapter 1), we find that, although our tools are crude, we are not reduced to saying nothing at all. We are able, with a little thoughtfulness, to begin to see how experience is structured. We can see why events of everyday life mean what they do to us. With relative clarity and simplicity, we find that we can use concepts developed in a tradition of European philosophy. These concepts also open onto the most profound philosophical problems of all time. That need not frighten us. Even if we wanted to explore the gigantic issues of ontology, we could do no better than to begin as we are—as somewhat clumsy and brazen psychologists trying to understand experience.

Chapters 1 and 2 engage us in a minute analysis and description of very common, unremarkable experiences. It is precisely the everyday and commonplace in experience that interests us most—those ways of seeing, behaving, and being that are so thoroughly taken for granted that we rarely question them. We do not have to turn to ecstatic or peak experiences to find something puzzling enough to interest us. A simple, everyday perception of anything embodies the most complex and intriguing challenges that psychology can take up. We do not understand, for example, how a chair over there can have a visual presence for us over here, how *it* is there and our knowledge of it is here, and how we can take the memory of it anywhere. Yet we *do* have *an* understanding of these phenomena, and that understanding *is* how the phenomena are possible. We lack a scientific understanding but assume an everyday understanding. Our attempt in this book will be to think scientifically (in the broad sense of that term) about our everyday lives.

In Chapter 2 we attempt to establish some conceptual tools, crude as they may be for now. These concepts may enable us to describe experience as it is lived, without distorting it in the process. The goal of this chapter is to describe some basic aspects of human experience, working our way up (or down) to the basic format of all our experiencing: *the fact that it always involves a world.* This development, from some basic aspects to the basic format, is recapitulated in Parts III and IV in more detail.

In Part II we interrupt this theoretical development with four chapters on the critical issues of method. My goal here is to persuade you that it is possible to do psychology phenomenologically. Some approaches, again from the philosophers, are described in Chapter 3, which deals with the general issues of understanding and communicating. In formulating these approaches we merely articulate what we all do more or less automatically in our everyday understanding of ourselves and others. Our goal as psychologists is always to take everyday experience, upon which psychology is inevitably based, and to make it as rigorous, systematic, and fruitful as possible.

In Chapter 4 we describe some approaches to research problems that have been adopted. These early attempts at phenomenological rigor in psychology lead us to ask how they can be improved. Chapter 5 takes up that question, focusing on the advantages and difficulties of asking people what we want to know from them instead of the more traditional methodology of merely observing their behavior. In Chapter 6 we draw out some suggestions for clinical method. Like Chapter 4, this chapter is selective. I hope to have offered a representative sample of techniques and approaches.

In Part III we offer a more detailed look at some of the steps covered in Chapter 2, the development of concepts. Chapters 7, 8, and 9 each deal with an aspect of experience—a context of meaning that is part of the whole of every lived experience. The sequence of these chapters is not important. Physical space and its physiognomic appearance, to which we orient ourselves bodily, supply one layer of meaning for all human experience (Chapter 7). A personal identity with a past and a future is a second implicit context from which experience always gains meaning (Chapter 8). Our network of interpersonal agreements is a third aspect; often subtle but powerful, this context is never absent from our lived experience (Chapter 9). To assert that experience is always physical, personal, and social is hardly astonishing. To say that we are going to unpack these subtleties and relate them to the data of lived experience may be not only astounding but also perhaps overambitious. But we rush in.

The three chapters of Part III are best read "experientially." That is, every statement, every concept, and every proposition ought to point to lived experience. The best concepts will do so automatically; others may require the reader to direct his attention to his experience to try to make a connection. The best way to grasp phenomenology is to begin right now being a phenomenologist. For every example I give, think of several of your own, and ask yourself whether my point describes your experience as it is lived by you. Each chapter should suggest to you a number of possible phenomenological analyses. Try them out; test your limits; be frustrated and let the frustration propel you into more clarity about experience. This book is written to be surpassed. The thoughtful reader will do so.

Part IV concludes the development of Part III with the concept of "world," much as Chapter 2 concludes, in a more preliminary way, with the same concept. Although the notion of "world" is our conclusion, it is perhaps better seen as the starting point. When we understand what it means to explore the lived world, we are ready to begin doing phenomenological psychology in a systematic and rigorous way. For the lived world is also the beginning of experience—its basis and fundamental horizon. To do phenomenological psychology rigorously, we must cut to the root—or better, to the ground—of experience as it is experienced every day by each one of us.

Again, this task is simultaneously very easy and very difficult. It is easy to see experience in this way because that is how experience is; there is no experience in the human enterprise that is not based on a fundamental sense of the world and of how we are in it. It is difficult to see experience this way because we are not accustomed to scrutinizing our experience so critically and reflectively. Most of our everyday lives are built upon unquestioned (some say unquestionable) assumptions. What experiences mean to us is usually so obvious that we do not feel the need to understand the sources and shapes of those meanings. Even natural science, one of man's most impressive achievements, does not interrogate experience (upon which it too is based) with systematic rigor. The attempt of phenomenology to do just that promises to be a contribution not only to psychology but also therefore to all science. In this book, however, we focus on psychology.

This primer is also written so that it can be read on two distinct levels. The text of the chapters contains as few references as possible to other writers and their struggles to develop the ideas I use. Beginning students can read the book while completely ignoring the footnotes. The only disadvantages of doing so are, first, that ideas that are not originally mine may appear to be mine, and, second, that larger issues and further questions the critical reader may ask are not taken up. There are notes at the end of the book for the reader who wants to correct these disadvantages. The historical status of the major concepts is mentioned, major philosophical contributions of phenomenology are briefly summarized, and numerous references are given. Finally, questions that the more critical reader may ask are taken up in the notes.

Lewisburg, Pennsylvania   E.K.
October 1974

CONTENTS

PART
I

INTRODUCTION

CHAPTER

1

A FIVE-YEAR-OLD
CHANGES HER MIND*

Let us watch my five-year-old daughter. She is carefully putting her pajamas, hairbrush, and favorite doll into a large paper sack. After this packing is done, she waits eagerly by the telephone for her friend to call to say that her supper is over and that they can now begin their overnight together. The telephone call comes. She is eager and happy as she puts on her coat, then grabs her sack in one arm and my hand with the other hand in order to walk to her friend's home, two houses down the street. The two girls giggle when they see each other, and together they run off to the bedroom.

Three quarters of an hour later we receive a phone call from her friend's mother. My daughter has been crying uncontrollably for half an hour and wants to come home. There is no apparent reason for this behavior; all she can say is that she wants to go home. As I bring her home, her tears subside, and when we come through the front door she grins. Even though we send her right to bed, she is glad to be home, and she does not cry further or demand a snack or a story. She goes right to sleep.

These are the broad outlines of the episode that will occupy us in this chapter, and we shall return to it many times throughout the book. Do we understand what happened here? I was puzzled by my daughter's behavior;

*This chapter was originally published, in a slightly different version, under the same title in the *Journal of Phenomenological Psychology*, 1973, 3, 161–171. Humanities Press, Inc., New Jersey.

I did not expect it to happen. Let us go through the events again, filling in some details and trying to reduce our puzzlement.

How can we understand this episode? My daughter's careful packing seems to have been done with a certain attitude, mood, expectation. The placing of articles in the sack may have been accompanied by her imagining that she would soon take them out again at her friend's house. It may also have been imitating packing she had seen her parents do. Or perhaps she was thinking of keeping things neat, as her mother had taught her to do with her bureau. Whatever she may specifically have been thinking while she packed—and it may have been all these things—the early part of the evening had a certain flavor, a taste of anticipation, of looking eagerly into a future of fun and pleasure.

And then things changed. Perhaps as she unpacked her sack, she thought of her parents, two houses away, cheerfully getting along without her. Maybe the distance between the houses loomed frighteningly large. Somehow the anticipation of a few minutes before was dead, and her present experience was quite different.

She may have remembered her usual bedtime routine: a snack, a story, kissing her mother good night, then snuggling down under the covers of a warm and familiar bed. Being with her good friend was somehow not as safe nor as comfortable as her memory of her own bed. All she could utter through her tears was that she wanted to go home.

And then, after returning home, a third distinct mood or attitude seems to have taken over. She looked briefly into her room, then ran to her bed and gratefully disappeared under the covers, demanding nothing further, and happy to be home. She went to sleep quickly and easily. Neither anticipations of what would soon happen nor memories of what usually happens seemed to be on her mind. She was appreciating the present moment just as it was. It felt good. Her loneliness of a few minutes earlier was no longer in force.

We do not know, of course, the precise details of her experience during the three stages of the evening. All we really have to go on is her behavior, as she made her desires known to us through language and action. Yet, if we could know these details, we would not find her behavior mysterious or puzzling. Perplexed as we might be at first, every motion and every word would make sense to us if we could know the thoughts and the feelings that accompanied them. How can we know these thoughts and feelings? How can we come to understand her behavior?

If we were not psychologists, we would simply settle for the explanation that she changed her mind. But, because we are psychologists, we demand of ourselves and our psychology that we understand what was involved in her changing her mind. What more might we be able to guess about her experience, so that we can understand better?

TIME

During the packing operation, my daughter was full of anticipation of her overnight. Placing articles carefully into the sack had a certain meaning for her, and we can see in her behavior some of that meaning. She wondered aloud how soon her friend would call. She wanted to be ready in time. Everything she experienced fell against the backdrop of her anticipation. And that backdrop of expectations for a fun-filled overnight made things mean what they did mean to her. She was living the anticipation, even while packing; she was living into the future, was pointed that way, and the future penetrated her present, giving it direction and meaning.

After she was at her friend's house, she changed her mind. Her *experience* changed. All she could say was that she wanted to come home. Was she frightened that something would happen at her friend's house? Probably not, for she had been there during the day many times and had always seemed to enjoy it. If she was frightened that something would happen, the fear was not present while she was packing. Indeed, it did not seem to be the future that flavored her experience after she changed her mind; it seemed instead to be the past. Home. She remembered it, and she wanted to be there. Its safety and familiarity seemed to call her back. She looked at her friend, the room, her sack, and they no longer *meant* to her a fun-filled overnight; rather they meant an inferior version of how she usually went to sleep. Her parents, not physically present, seemed nevertheless to be psychologically present. Her memory of them made their physical absence intolerable. The past, not the future, provided the backdrop for her experience of events, and these events took on a very different meaning. Indeed, the structure of her experience was very different at this stage. She was living her memories; she was living back into the past, and that was the direction toward which she was pointed. She very efficiently produced behavior that would achieve an approximation of that past.

Both these experiences, living into the future and living into the past, were discernibly different from how she experienced her room and bed upon returning home. The present, in its immediate presence, is penetrated by neither future nor past but is complete in itself, as it is, and she was absorbed in it.

There remain a number of unanswered questions about my daughter's episode, like why her experience changed as it did. Why did she change her mind? Before broaching that question, however, we really ought to understand what she was experiencing as well as we can. What really changed was the quality of her experience, its meaning. And a good deal of descriptive work has to be done before we shall be able to discern what things meant to her as she was going through the phases of the evening.

A critical problem for psychologists, as they try to do such descriptive work, is that there is no well-developed language in terms of which to make the description clear. We know *that* events mean things to people, and we know that *what* the events mean determines our reactions. But we do not know very much about the origin or production of meaning itself.[1]

In our descriptive attempts we have tried to show how the events of the evening were meaningful because of the backdrops against which they appeared. Furthermore, we tried to show how various *time zones*–past, present, and future–provided such backdrops. Before my daughter left home, the sack (for example) was experienced against the backdrop of her eager anticipations, and it *meant* a fun-filled overnight. After she was in the other house a while, the same sack was experienced against the backdrop of her fond memories of home. It *meant* an unpleasantly inferior version of how she usually goes to sleep.

Living into the future is a reckoning of the meaning of present events in terms of our anticipations. Living into the past is a reckoning of the meaning of events in terms of our memories. In such experiences, the past and future literally permeate the present; they invade in a total way and pre-empt the meanings of, the very perceptions of, current events. Such experiential phenomena are not random; they have a definite structure, and that structure would be revealed as orderly, if only we could carry our descriptive work far enough to see it clearly.

It is important to see that when time zones are the backdrops, future and past penetrate the present in much more complex ways than we have yet described. My daughter's anticipation of a fun-filled overnight was based upon memories, like the good times she had had with her friend and what she recalled of her friend's room, where she was looking forward to sleeping. What she was looking forward to appeared in her experience against the backdrop of what she looked back to: events against the backdrop of anticipations and anticipations against the backdrop of memories— a complex structure, but entirely relevant to our task of understanding her behavior in the first stage of the evening (see Figure 1).

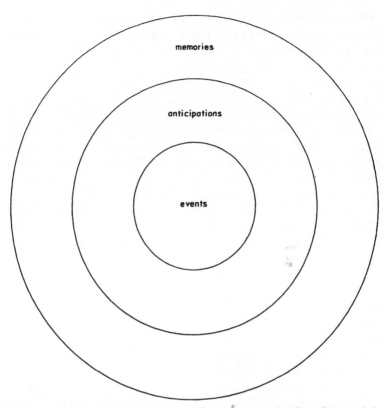

Figure 1. The Structure of Temporal Experience in the First Phase of the Evening.   Events like packing the sack have meaning because of the *anticipation* of a fun-filled overnight, which is the experiential context, or backdrop, for the activity. Anticipations, in turn, appear against the backdrop of *remembering* previous fun with friends, which gives the anticipations their meaning.

As she was crying, wanting to come home, her memory of home made the sack, the bed, and the room appear lonely, alien, unwelcome. But the memory of home loomed only because of a further backdrop of anticipation—of going to sleep in this alien room. She had been in the room many times before and had not found it unbearable. But knowing that she was supposed to go to sleep there made the room appear an empty place, a cold place, in contrast to her memory of her own warm bed at home. She would not have remembered her own bed except for the prior anticipation of sleeping in this one. Events against the backdrop of memories and memories against the backdrop of anticipations also provide a complex structure, schematized in Figure 2.

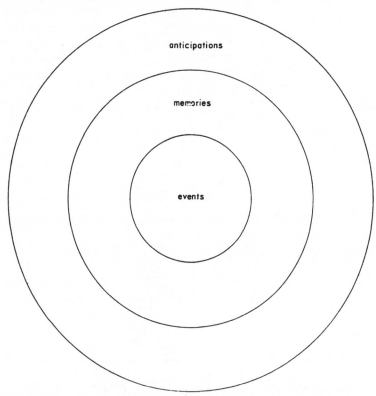

Figure 2. The Structure of Temporal Experience in the Second Phase of the Evening.   Events like looking around the friend's room have their meaning because of the memory of home, which, in contrast to the perception of the friend's room, offers warmth, familiarity, and safety. This memory, however, becomes salient only because of the further backdrop of anticipation, of staying in the friend's room all night.

It is difficult to tell what came first, what started it all—the past as remembered or the future as anticipated. Indeed in experience, in contrast to the sequence of physical events in physical time reckoned by clocks, the future (as anticipated) may precede the past (as remembered). Here is one of the differences between the world of experience and the world as interpreted according to the traditions of the physical sciences.

As if these facts of experience did not make matters complex enough, we must mention that some memories are anticipated ("I shall always remember my bed back home") and that some anticipations are remembered ("I remember how I looked forward to this"). How can we find a way to bring order into the seemingly endless complexities of human experience? For now let us settle for the recognition that the meaning of events as they appear in our experience is heavily influenced by the temporal context in which they occur. The term "backdrops" of anticipation and memory is merely a way of indicating how those temporal contexts enter into the fabric of meaning—not as focal points, but as a ground against which figures appear, as in visual perception.

SPACE

Let us look again at my daughter's evening, this time in terms of the backdrop of *experiential space.* Let us see if we can discover more of what events meant to her. While she was concentrating on her packing, she was quietly talking to herself. Her face was going through a series of expressions, as if she were in a conversation. Suddenly she noticed me looking at her, her "conversation" stopped, and she gave me a big grin—only a little embarrassed that I had been watching her. Here we can see two distinct spaces, within which she "staged" her experience, one after the other. At first, the placing of articles within the bag occurred within a space occupied by herself, the task, and at least one other person, who was present to her but not to me. The "fantasy other" may have been her friend, her mother, or even her future husband. We would not know who it was unless she were to tell us, but it is clear that she was construing her actions according to a *social field,* a space structured by (1.) herself as worker on the task, (2.) the task itself as a display for the other, and (3.) the other as an audience and fantasy commentator on her performance. She was very much involved in the dynamics of this space when she suddenly noticed me watching her (see Figure 3).

She was too young to be as self-conscious about fantasy as the rest of us are, but, as soon as she noticed me watching, the spatial context, and hence the meaning, of the events changed abruptly. She was a little embarrassed—because I saw her having the fantasy. I became an other in her experience, and the space was now occupied by (1.) her as the one who has just been watched without knowing it; (2.) the events, including both the actions and the fantasy; and (3.) myself, the observer (see Figure 4). She

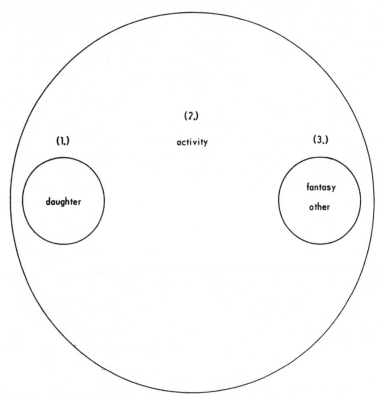

Figure 3. The Social Field in Which the Fantasy Took Place.   Note that my daughter's activity is oriented toward the other in a display. The fantasy other is, in her experiential field, watching her activity and commenting on it. This activity is therefore *social,* even though no real others are included; she does not notice my watching, and I am not part of the field.

may have thought that I knew the content of her other space, or she may possess a solid sense of her own privacy of thought and knows that she can keep things from me. But it did not matter much because she trusts me and has not yet learned to be ashamed of her imagination.

These two spaces provided the events of her experience with some of the meaning they had for her. They were like contexts or stages upon which the events were played out. These spaces were temporary, however, and appeared against a larger background of the space marked off geographically by the two houses and populated with two groups: her family at home and her friend and her friend's family in the other house. Were it

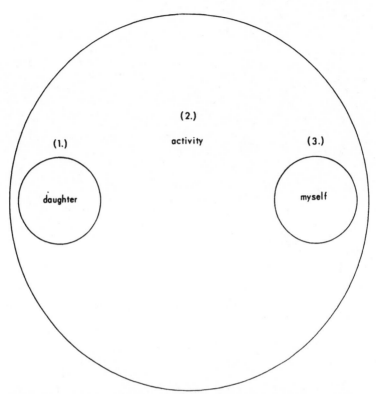

Figure 4. The Social Field as Soon as My Daughter Sees Me Watching Her.
This social field differs from that in Figure 3 in that the other, myself, is
real instead of fantasied. My daughter surely knows the difference between real and fantasied others, yet the activity of packing is neither more
nor less *social* here than in Figure 3—from the point of view of her experience and what events meant to her.

not for that larger space or something like it, it would have been totally
meaningless to put things in the sack, wait for the telephone, and so on.

As she awaited the call, the two houses stood as opposite poles in a two-
pole field. Her own house represented ordinary, dull routine, and the pros-
pect of staying another minute seemed unpleasant. Two doors away, in
contrast, were the shining rooms of her friend's house, where fun would
take place. She could feel the pull of the other house as she stood in her
own, looking at the door and the telephone, then wandering around idly
fingering familiar things (see Figure 5).

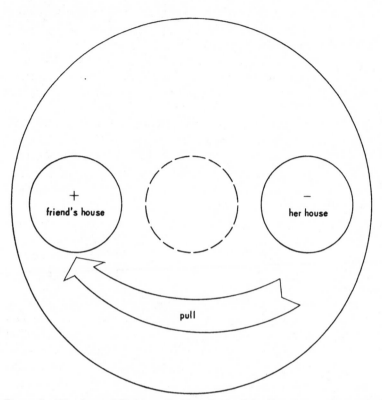

Figure 5. The Spatial Field in the First Part of the Evening.   The pull of
the friend's house is symbolized by the arrow, which in turn traverses her
anticipated path of movement. Her anticipations probably included tra-
versing this distance and obeyed the environmental attraction as structured
in her experience. The + and – signs indicate the same vector. This diagram
is merely reversed for the second part of the evening.

We know that after she was in the other house for a while the values of
the poles in this two-pole field shifted. The friend's house became alien,
and home was "home." The pull was in the opposite direction. When we
ask why she "changed her mind," we must specify what changed in her
"mind" before we can broach the question. One of the things that changed
was the structure of the space that included the two houses. The attractive
one became unattractive, and the unattractive one became attractive. The
experience of the friend's house, upon her first arriving there, fell against
the backdrop of space as originally structured. Later her experience of the

same house was utterly transformed. The shining rooms shone differently; they looked different, felt different, and had a different meaning. That difference was possible because the structure of the space against which they were experienced had become reversed. The rooms that had been shining promises of fun became alien territory. They did not look different to *me,* but they had a presence in *her* experience that was what it was only because the structure of the entire space changed.

Or did the structure of the larger space change *because* the rooms in her friend's house came to look different? It is not, I think, a matter of causality, in which one change caused the other. The changing of her "mind" was a changing of all these things at once. What is critical is that events, objects, and people came to *mean something different* to her; the origin of meaning in experience is the context within which events, objects, and people appear—the backdrops that allow them to stand out and be experienced. In understanding her change of mind, we are therefore seeking to understand her change of meanings, and, in understanding her change of meanings, we seek to articulate the experiential contexts of events from which meanings emerge.

We are still some distance from understanding why she changed her mind, but we are certainly closer than when we first puzzled over the question, because we know something of *what* changed. Meanings changed, and they changed because (along with) the very structure of her experience changing. Particularly, we may say that she shifted from a future to a past and finally to a present orientation, and we may say that the values of attraction and repulsion in a two-poled space reversed themselves.

In order to arrive at an understanding of why she changed her mind, it is often useful to ask why we ask the question. The question seems important to us because my daughter's behavior was different from the way that we see ourselves behaving. I would not make plans with other people and then, for reasons that I know would remain mysterious to them, change my mind and disappoint them. Such behavior is not polite. Part of the importance of the question comes from a sense of a difference between my daughter and myself. I am usually not arrested by the behavior of others when it is similar to my own. Perhaps we ought, however, as psychologists, to be as interested in "understandable" behavior as in "puzzling" behavior.

But what is the difference between my daughter and myself? The impoliteness of her behavior did not impress her; she did not experience her behavior as impolite. Why not? Because she characteristically structures her experience differently from the way in which I structure mine. Her way of experiencing herself in space and time "permits" such changes of mind, whereas mine does not. The difference is twofold, temporal and spatial. First, the temporal: My anticipations of fun would have made the experience more fun than it was for her. My remembered anticipations ("I recall how I've looked forward to this") would have colored my seeing the expected rooms, providing my experience with more ballast than was available to her. Furthermore, I would be "ashamed of myself" for changing my mind, which she obviously was not. Anticipating that I would remember the incident (anticipated memories) and continue to be ashamed of it would have deterred my behaving as she did. So, in relation to both anticipated memories and remembered anticipations, meanings in my experience would have been more stable. These additional complexities—the relevance of anticipated memories and remembered anticipations—may well be the products of learned or natural maturation, and they may represent a critical difference between five-year-old and adult experiential structures[2] (see Figure 6).

Even if I were to have allowed myself the change of *meanings* that my daughter experienced, however, I would probably not have *acted* as she did. I would have been more sensitive to the impoliteness of the act and to the disappointment that I would cause in others. I would have been "ashamed of myself," and shame emerges from an interpersonal field. The second difference between my own and my daughter's experiential structures is thus *spatial*.

Shame, as commonly understood, requires an other in whose eyes we feel judged. Such an experience necessarily engages us in a space that is somehow different from that of my daughter. In shame, the space in which the experience occurs and the context that allows it to mean what it means are intensely interpersonal. Events that we are ashamed of happen in a space in which there is at least one other whose judgment counts—else we would not experience them as shameful.[3]

It is not that my daughter, at age five years, is incapable of experiencing shame. A few years ago she was incapable, but now she is capable of the mild embarrassment that I saw when she discovered me watching her fantasy and that involves a spatial context similar to that of shame (see Figure 4).

But she was not ashamed that she had changed her mind as she did. Such a space was not a relevant context for, and it did not determine the meaning of, her decision to change her mind as she did.

Therefore, it is not the absence, but rather the relative weakness, of this experiential structure that makes her different from myself and most other

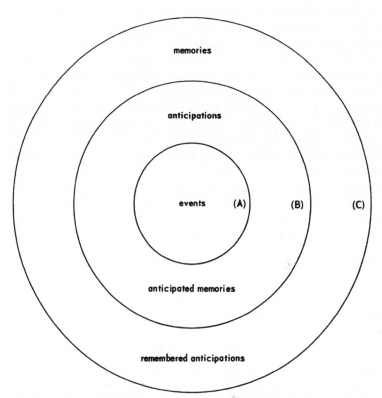

Figure 6. Adult Anticipation. This adult experiential structure includes, in the anticipatory backdrop (B) to events (A), an anticipation of remembering my shame if I change my mind; it is therefore less likely to shift to the arrangement in Figure 2, as it did for my daughter. It also includes, in the memory backdrop (C) to anticipations (B), a remembering of how I looked forward to these events, which would also lend this structure more stability.

adults. Under special circumstances, for example, if we had tried to make her ashamed of what she did, she could have experienced shame. But in this instance she did not. Perhaps the remarkable thing to learn from this episode is not so much about her experience as it is about our own adult experience. There is practically nothing in adult experience of everyday life that does not derive some of its meaning from a context of interpersonal space. Nearly all our behavior occurs within a *contract* or *agreement*, explicit or implicit, and we are constantly aware, at the margin of our experience, of this context. Indeed, events mean to us, as adults, what they do largely because of this interpersonal backdrop against which they stand out as events, experiences, at all.[4]

Five-year-old experience does not have quite this character, and so we see how my daughter's "change of mind" was possible for her in a way that it would not be for us as adults. Her experience had neither the stability of adult experience lent by the complexities of remembered anticipations and anticipated memories, nor the stability lent by a more or less constant context of interpersonal contracts and agreements in which the other's point of view is part of what events mean to us and we assume that the other's point of view is stable.

We may, however, be more specific in saying something about why my daughter changed her mind, if we can see the change within the context of the way in which she structures her experience in general. We know from other behavior that she understands herself to be a young version of her mother (she plays with dolls, dishes, and so on). Although this perspective is important from the point of view of the outrageous ubiquity of sexist role training, our main point here is that her mother is an adult who makes plans, including plans to have a good time, and then carries them out. When her mother plans, of course, she does so within an experiential structure that is adult, including the contractual character of which we have spoken, and the complexity of anticipated memories and remembered anticipations that enable her to sustain an adult kind of experiential stability. In my daughter's various imitations of her mother, including the plan for a fun-filled overnight, she does not have these supporting experiential structures. She does have, however, a five-year-old's knowledge of what such planning is, and, just as she imitates in doll play and dish play, she seeks to be like her mother in making plans.

Such imitation is anticipation on its grandest scale. There is a future-orientation *fundamentally built into* my daughter's understanding of herself as a young version of her mother. Such grand living-into-the-future provided a fundamental temporal backdrop against which the entire episode was experienced by my daughter and was meaningful. It was a context that lay behind the original context of living into the future as she awaited the telephone call. A context that involves our very definition of ourselves is a basic context indeed. Part of the meaning of her entire plan, therefore, was that she was becoming a big girl or, even more seriously, an adult, like her parents (see Figure 7).

By the time my daughter had changed her mind, it was clear to all concerned that she had overextended herself. In her temporal shift from future

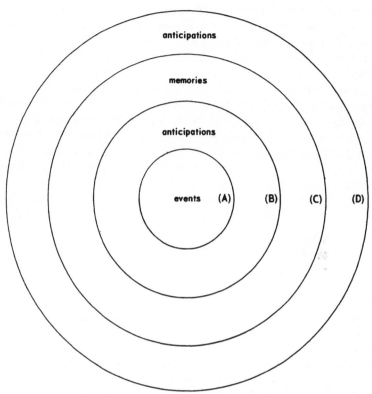

Figure 7. The Larger Structure of the Experience of the Whole Episode.
This diagram merely puts Figure 1 into a larger context, which enables us
to see other meanings of the events for my daughter. Her packing the sack
and other events in the first part of the evening (A) acquired part of their
meaning because they occurred against the backdrop of anticipating the
making and carrying out of plans (B), which was meaningful because of her
remembering how her mother makes and carries out plans (C). This memory was meaningful in turn because she anticipates being an adult like her
mother (D).

to past orientation and her spatial shift from centrifugal to centripital
attractions, the underlying context of meanings, growing up, became irrelevant. In its place the past appeared as the determiner of meanings and
indeed, as another part of her implicit understanding of herself: "I am a
child." This shift occurred, and she changed her mind, we can now say,
because she had overextended herself. Fortunately, her "growing up" is

not her only available self-understanding. When her experience could not sustain the anticipation of a fun-filled overnight, she was not crushed and obliterated by her failure. She was quite content to be a little girl. She was, as all children are, ahead of herself but not totally committed to the advance.

At least this time she was not. On some future occasion, when growing up has become even more important as a backdrop to determine the meaning of events and when the interpersonal space of shame has become a more constant context of her experience, more may be at stake. Failure will be more costly, but success will be more likely, after the contractual sense has become a more stable part of her experience, after the complexities of remembered anticipations and anticipated memories supply her with more ballast for the stability of meanings, and after her definition of herself as a little girl becomes less available as a frame of meaning within which to understand herself.

It is interesting to note that, whereas our phenomenological analysis has given us a pretty good idea of *why* my daughter changed her mind and *what* changed when she did, we have really discovered nothing that we did not already know. Yet at the beginning of the study we were puzzled in a way that we are not now puzzled. The fact that I already "knew" everything written here is revealed in my impulse to try to correct the awkward situation created by the incident: the impulse to say such things as "What will the neighbors think?"; "How have you made your friend feel?" (the social context of behavior and experience); "You will be sorry tomorrow!" (anticipated memories); "An hour ago you could hardly wait!" (remembered anticipations); "Don't you want to be a big girl?"; "Don't be a baby!" (self-definitions as meaning-producing contexts). This impulse was to make her see the matter as we do, implicitly knowing that she was experiencing it differently. We knew it all, but we did not know *what* we knew or that we knew it. For that reason we were puzzled.[5]

Phenomenology does not yield new information in the way that science pushes back the frontiers of knowledge. Its task is less to give us new ideas than to make explicit those ideas, assumptions, and implicit presuppositions upon which we already behave and experience life. Its task is to reveal to us exactly what we already know and that we know it, so that we can be less puzzled about ourselves. Were it to tell us something that we did not know, it would not be telling us anything about ourselves, and therefore it would not be important.[6]

CHAPTER
2

BEHAVIOR AND
BEING-IN-THE-WORLD

It is apparent from the analysis in Chapter 1 that phenomenological psychology seeks to clarify our experience. Conscious experience is a critical part of the psychology of human beings.[1] One way to clarify experience is to seek what events *mean* to us. In asking this question, we discover that conscious experience has a certain *structure*. Indeed, we might say that the "structuredness" of experience *is* the meaningfulness of experience. Structureless experience would be a meaningless experience. The structure of experience is more or less implicit, but it is absolutely critical for the meanings that events have for us. Or, stated more accurately, because meaning *is* structure, we should say that *meaning* is more or less implicit in experience. Phenomenological psychology seeks to articulate explicitly the implicit structure and meaning of human experience.

In order to carry out this task, we must *describe* experience.[2] Any description highlights only what its terms allow, and so our choice of descriptive terms is critical for our task. In Chapter 1 a number of terms and relations were used. Let us first examine them and then introduce further terms that can help to fulfill our task. How can we describe the structure of experience?

In Chapter 1 events were said to appear in experience against a backdrop. Phenomenologists call such a backdrop a *horizon*.[3] This backdrop, or horizon, is not usually the focus of our attention, yet it is clearly decisive for what things mean to us. My daughter would not have awaited her friend's telephone call so eagerly if it had not already acquired some meaning. The meaning it had was based upon her anticipation of a fun-filled overnight. We are therefore saying that anticipations can (always do?) give meaning as backdrop or horizon. Memories, too, as we come to understand the second part of my daughter's evening, can be seen to be (always are?) a horizon that gives meaning to current events. Furthermore, every horizon *has* a horizon; that is, a horizon means what *it* means only because of the backdrop against which *it* appears. My daughter's anticipation of the fun-filled overnight was an anticipation of fun only because she had memories of fun with her friend, which supplied her anticipation with some meaning.

When we pay attention to our ordinary experience, we notice that it sometimes has a very sharp focus, as when we are reading a book. There are other times of undisciplined wandering, idly picking out this and that in the auditory or visual environment, then moving through memories and anticipations—apparently at random. Most of our experience lies somewhere between these two extremes. Whatever our degree of focus, our experiencing is a process of giving meanings to events—sometimes events in the environment, sometimes events in our own minds. If we can understand how it happens, we shall be able to put the apparently random events of consciousness into an order. Indeed, experience *is* ordered, but the structure and order of experience are difficult to describe. In our descriptive work so far, we have used the term *background* or *horizon,* and we have said that there are at least two kinds of horizons: temporal and spatial. There are surely others, and the entire lot of them operate simultaneously. Events always mean many things to us at once, just as my daughter's visit to her friend's house meant a fun-filled overnight, a recapitulation of previous experiences of fun, obeying the pushes and pulls of environmental space, and being a "big girl" who could make plans and carry them out as her parents do—to mention only a few.

How are the various meanings in our experience, the various horizons, related to one another? In Chapter 1 the temporal structuring of experience seemed to exist alongside the spatial one. Furthermore, one spatial horizon, which emerges from the pushes and pulls of the physiognomy of the environment, seems to exist alongside the spatial horizon structured by interpersonal contracts, obligations, expectations, and so on. Finally, there is the horizon reflecting how my daughter understands herself as a person: first as a young version of adults who make plans and carry them out and later as content to be a little girl.

All these meanings are organized in some way. What is the principle of this organization? What is the overall structure of experience? We may put this question in another way: What are the relations among horizons? If every horizon *has* a horizon, where does it all end? What is the ultimate horizon of human being against which all other horizons are staged, and in the context of which all events make sense to us?[4] Phenomenological philosophers have often written of the *ground* of meaning. Presumably, if the ground of meaning were clear, the principle of organization of horizons would be easier to see.

In trying to describe the overall structure of experience, we must look to experience itself. What is experience itself like? As I sit at my desk, the space in front of me is filled with familiar objects. The room spreads out before me in an orderly way. That is, the book on my desk is the book I have been trying to understand for a couple of days. It lies there, full of meanings for me—such meanings as my memory of its contents, my sense of where it stands in relation to my own work, and my sense of myself as having a work, part of which is to understand the book. Other books line the walls. They have a place in the room, and the room has a place in my life. Pictures of my children sit on my desk. They are my children, and I am their father. Knowing them makes their pictures part of a meaningful experience of the room. I remember when they were smaller and anticipate when they will be bigger. These temporal horizons blend with the spatial horizon of the desk top on which they sit to make a meaningful whole. Pencils, with which I anticipate writing about the book I shall read, lie spatially and temporally in front of me. The entire experience is an orderly whole, of which temporal and spatial horizons are analytically separable aspects. The experience as it is *lived* absorbs all the horizons that we have discussed into a unity of my being-in-my-office.[5] In the diagrams of horizons we have *analytically* separated certain horizons for consideration. Lived experience *synthesizes*[6] them all, as in my concrete presence to the room and its presence to me.

This *lived experience* must be our guide in understanding other people and what things mean to them. Although we may separate horizons analytically and diagram them in layers, the layers were all integrated in my daughter's experience of the inside of her house, for example, in the first part of her evening. The room spread out before her as mine does now. It meant all the things we have said it meant, yet it appeared not as layers or diagrams but rather as the inside of her house. Experience is creative; it synthesizes all the horizons that we have mentioned, plus the objective presence of tables, chairs, telephones, and people, into a *meaningful field* spread out before her, within which she moves according to the purpose or intention that she has within the field. A *field* is a perceptual space, present right now, already meaningful, with layers of meaning, integrating multiple horizons into a coherent present moment of being-in-a-field.

But we must look somewhat farther for more basic horizons if we are to see why my daughter's being-in-a-field was as it was that night. We found that the implicit *notion that she had of herself* was a horizon more fundamental than her specific anticipations and memories. This horizon gave her anticipations and memories their meanings. It was surely a *more implicit* horizon, one that she would not think of herself. In the same way, one layer of meaning for me in writing these sentences is the implicit sense of who I am and where I am in my life history. Writing these sentences would not mean to me what it does if I understood myself to be an adolescent or a lawyer. We may say that we can understand what something means to someone only if we can see *his* implicit sense of who he is, which is a critical horizon against which events appear to that person and gain their meanings.

Therefore, the horizon of who my daughter thinks she is also gave her experience of her field *its* meaning. When we think about the fields within which our behavior occurs and toward which it is pointed, we note that everyday life is a sequence of contemporaneous fields. We move from room to room, from inside to outside, from one group of people to another to being alone. These fields are spatial, but their space is organized in our experience partly according to who we think we are. If I am a professor and I walk into the student union of a university, my perception of the interior of that building, especially in its interpersonal and social aspect, is influenced by my sense of myself as a professor. If you are a student and you walk into a professor's office, the office space will be structured differently for you than for him. Behind the desk is *his* place; other chairs are *yours*. The physiognomy of the environment of that room produces definite pushes and pulls. It seems awkward to sit in his chair; if he is berating you, the door leading out pulls. You can feel the pull physically.

WORLD

Being who one thinks one is in a field must be clarified further. Figure 5 in Chapter 1 maps my daughter's field geographically; Figures 3 and 4 map fields interpersonally, and we can even describe my daughter's sense of herself as a little girl who is growing up as a kind of temporal field. These fields are horizons, but they are also organized in experience in some way.

We do not become totally different people as we move from one environment, one interpersonal context, or one sense of self as growing to another. This higher level of organization of fields into a *world* is a more basic horizon of any particular field. That is, *world* is where we are most fundamentally. My orientation to the world is the most basic horizon from which I derive meanings for my experience. Who I am in the world determines what fields will be salient, what they will mean to me, and how they will influence the meanings of events in my experience.[7]

My orientation to the world in general, like (even more than) other horizons, is implicit in my experience. Although it is the most fundamental horizon of my life, it is rarely called into question, brought into focus, or described. Who-I-am-in-the-world is the gigantic assumption upon which I rely in order for my experience to be meaningful at all to me.[8] Even when I question who I am in the world, I still sustain the identity of a person-in-the-world who is seeking his place. *World* is always there; if it were to go away somehow, experience would veer off into a meaningless jumble and become nonsense. That rarely happens to most of us.[9]

Let us return to my daughter's episode and see how the notion of *world* can take us farther in understanding it. At the end of Chapter 1 we were able to see that all the meanings embedded in her anticipations and memories and in her spatial fields were based upon her implicit understanding of herself as a little girl growing up. The first part of her evening, in which she was full of anticipation of fun, was also an enactment of growing up as she understood it. The second part of her evening, in which she was full of memories of home, was an enactment of being a little girl.[10] Both of these enactments were played out in a larger, even more implicit context of her understanding of herself as our daughter, her friend's friend, a resident of one house, a visitor in another, her brother's sister, her neighbor's neighbor's daughter, and so on. That is, her parents, her friend, her home, the other house, her brothers, the neighbors—all these elements are part of her *world*. These contextual elements form a whole, a pattern of coherence, within which events are intelligible to her. All the meanings we have been able to see meant what they did only because of this coherent world within which they took place. Visiting, coming home, growing up, being a little girl—each meant what it meant to her because she already understood herself as being-in-the-world. The bag she packed, the rooms she saw, the paths she traversed, the people she was with were all meaningful events because she is sane, human, and in possession of an understanding of herself as being-in-the-world. Being-in-the-world is the largest and final context, or horizon, that she depends on; to understand her perceptions and her actions in the context of her being-in-the-world is to understand the episode in its most basic, human, and vital sense.

If I perceive a book and want to understand what is happening in my perception, I must look at that perception and try to understand the meanings inherent in it. I do not perceive color, shape, and so on as a meaningless jumble. I experience the book, lying there on the table three feet away, within reach and "beckoning" me to open it, which is possible because my hands are free and I am situated comfortably on a chair, placed in front of a desk, by the window, upstairs in my house, down the block from my place of work, and so on. All these aspects are relevant, indeed essential to, the perception of the book. I could not perceive the book in an empty space, devoid of myself and my purposes—my being-in-the-world. All these elements are aspects of the horizon of world, and it is quite unthinkable for me to have a conscious experience of the book without also having a world to put it in, within which it is a meaningful event. The structure of my particular world, my tasks and purposes, however I construe them, are necessary for there to be a book at all. There is no worldless book. Similarly, as my daughter took up her world in the making of plans, pajamas and hairbrush appeared in her perceptual field. They were not "just there"; rather, they were part of her world of anticipation as she had structured it at the time. They had meaning. There are no worldless pajamas either.

We must understand my daughter, her perceptions, and her actions in this sense because she understands them in this sense. Indeed, to experience an event in some relation to the world we know is what we generally mean by "understanding" at all. My daughter's understanding, of course, is implicit for her. We can make it explicit for ourselves and say that we really understand, but we already understood it implicitly ourselves even before we started the analysis. We already knew, as soon as we first heard the story, some of what was going on. We understood her desire to visit, then her desire to come home, because we too, like my daughter, have an implicit sense of being-in-the-world. But by making explicit the understanding that is implicit we relieve ourselves of a sense of puzzlement, anger, or whatever else may have motivated our exploration.

BEHAVIOR

If we understand world as a fundamental horizon and if we understand that my daughter understands herself as being-in-the-world, what can we now say about her *behavior?* Both my daughter's perceptions and her actions were *expressions* of her being-in-the-world.[11] To understand her in this way is to understand her in the ways that she is essentially *like everyone else.* Every person has a being-in-the-world. To understand her *in her uniqueness* or this particular episode in its particularity, we must understand her unique world and how she is uniquely in it. How can we understand her unique world? The world is a complex of interrelated meanings—for my daughter, for myself, and for all of us. To specify, as we have, some of the horizons that made events meaningful to her and some of the ways in which she construed her field at the time is to begin to paint a portrait of her unique world. The world in which we find ourselves is already meaningful, and to interpret our perceptions and actions as *expressions* of our being-in-the-world is to understand perceptions and actions as they are—in their already meaningful state.

Amid the rich complexity of behavior, especially human behavior, the task of understanding is monumental. It seems hopeless, in fact, until we realize that, even without discipline and training, the most naïve of us already does understand a great deal. Countless behaviors are observed by me every minute I am with people, and these behaviors are immediately intelligible to me. To feel that I don't understand is sufficiently rare that it provokes a conscious, problem-solving attitude, an aim to bring me back to understanding.

When we began our analysis, we both understood and did not understand. We understood that my daughter is a particular being-in-the-world (though we did not call it that)—that is, that she shares with us a common environment and interprets it in a way similar to our own. We knew that events mean something to her—though we were not sure precisely what they meant. We knew that she organizes her perceptions of the moment into a perceptual field with many meanings—though we were not sure *how* her perceptions are organized. We knew that she organizes these meanings into a coherent definition of herself as some part of the world—though we were not sure precisely how that looks to her, or at least we did not think about it explicitly. We knew, in general, that she is a *person* and shares with us all these things because all people do. That is what people are like. We knew she is a being-in-the-world.

But we were also puzzled by her specific behavior. I myself was a bit surprised. I did not know precisely how she interpreted events, or else I would not have been surprised. Our investigation in Chapter 1 was aimed at sharpening the precision of our already existing understanding. It was aimed at taking her behavioral expressions of her being-in-the-world and

understanding them in terms of her *particular* being-in-the-world, and at
understanding her particular being-in-the-world in terms of her *expressions.*

When we are understanding others, what we understand is their being-
in-the-world. To see another's behavior in some other way is to give it a
meaning that it does not have. To see it in the wrong context is to misunderstand. If I gesture for you to come here and you understand me to
be thumbing my nose, you will see my gesture as thumbing my nose, and
you will misunderstand. If you expect me to gesture for you to come here
and I actually thumb my nose, then you will either see the motion as asking
you to come, or you will be surprised. If you are surprised, it will not be
because of the muscle movements *per se* but because of their meaning,
which is reckoned in terms of my being-in-the-world. That is, you will have
to change your notion of how you fit into my world. It is on this level that
you will have learned something. Similarly, because I expected my daughter
to enjoy a fun-filled overnight, I was surprised by her behavior. I learned
something, and I learned because I was able to see her behavior in terms of
its meaning: What I learned was something of how she structures her
world—how she is-in-the-world.

UNCONSCIOUS BEHAVIOR

Sometimes my own behavior surprises me. The operative field that my
behavior expresses is sometimes different from the way I represent myself,
my being-in-the-world, to myself. It happens more or less frequently that
what we are doing and what we think we are doing are different. The
hysterical patient who vomits all his mother's cooking, but that of no one
else, may not know that he is expressing something about his self-mother
field. Indeed, his conscious intention may be to love his mother totally;
the last thing he wants may be to offend her. The pubescent boy who
wets his bed may be quite unaware of the operative field within which that
behavior is intelligible, and he and the urologist may agree that there is
surely something wrong with his urinary apparatus. Because such "unconscious" behavior is ubiquitous, the *experience* to which we must appeal in
order to understand it may well not be the most superficial level of highly
articulate ideas that we have about ourselves. Indeed, experience is layered,
with many horizons operating simultaneously. Our verbal or explicit presentation may be somewhat inaccurate or grossly misleading; the implicit
but operative field nevertheless will control our perceptions and actions.[12]

My daughter's behavior probably surprised her—though she barely remembered her poignant anticipations after she had changed her mind. In this episode we see a sequence of fields, rather than the simultaneous presence of two opposing ones, as in the instance of the boy who vomits his mother's food (love mother/hate mother). Suppose that my daughter were older, remembered her anticipations, had to save face in the interpersonal contract, and had a larger investment in her identity as "growing up"—yet still had the irresistible urge to return home that night. She, too, would have found it necessary to "get sick" (to develop vomiting, stomach ache, or something of that order) in order to go home. Such a maneuver, common in people older than she, would have allowed token recognition of her "official" presentation of herself to herself and to others while allowing her to express her being-in-the-world as it really was.[13]

DOING PSYCHOLOGY PHENOMENOLOGICALLY

Let us summarize what we have said about behavior. We have said that behavior is an expression of being-in-the-world. We mean that how one is-in-the-world controls his behavior, that being-in-the-world is what is revealed in his behavior, that what we understand when we understand behavior is the being-in-the-world that it expresses, and that it is only in the context of being-in-the-world that behavior is intelligible to us. These four propositions describe something of the overall approach of a phenomenological psychology.

Our analysis of my daughter's episode is an attempt to specify the structure of her being-in-the-world. The behavior that we observe in others is always interpreted by us in some way. By interpreting it in terms of a person's being-in-the world, we achieve an understanding better than, or at least different from, the interpretations of other popular kinds of psychology. By interpreting it phenomenologically, we are expanding what we already do in everyday experience by making it explicit. We are using our natural interpretations in more disciplined form.

What interpretive equipment have we gathered so far along the way? A phenomenological analysis of any piece of behavior can be carried out by anyone who is willing to try to understand. We may inquire, *first*, into the structure of the individual's experience of *time*. Does anticipation or memory seem to be the immediate backdrop of the events in their meaning to him? Is he, in his behavior, living primarily into the future or into the past? Whatever the immediate backdrop is, it has a meaning for him because of further horizons of a temporal nature—memories and anticipations. Understanding these horizons and how they are related to one another is an essential part of understanding his behavior.

We may inquire, second, into the physiognomic pushes and pulls of his immediate environment. How is his perceptual and behavioral *field*, within which his actions are oriented, structured? Where are the attractions and repulsions? In terms of the concrete behavioral space of a particular action, this inquiry yields only a description of the behavior. But behavior becomes revealing in that physical movement expresses. We also have to formulate *what* is being expressed, and this effort engages us in an inquiry into who he thinks he is within that field, how much the concrete field influences who he thinks he is, and how much who he thinks he is influences the appearance of the concrete field.

The spatial mapping of the behavioral field is not really independent of our first inquiry into the individual's experience of time. His concrete behavioral space will be interpreted by him in terms of an anticipation of a future locus in that space, a memory of a past one, or both. Or his behavior may be aimed at a restructuring of the space: He may physically move things around in it, putting up barriers and opening up channels of visual or auditory communication with other elements in that space.

We may also use the notion of a behavioral field less concretely and more metaphorically. My daughter may have wanted to move "closer" to her friend not just physically but emotionally as well. To move closer to her friend physically may have been a way to move closer emotionally to her mother—if, for example, her mother had led her to believe that she (mother) would love her more if she (daughter) were to stay all night with her friend.

Thinking spatially is therefore also not independent of a *third* line of inquiry: into interpersonal contracts, agreements, conflicts, desires to help or be helped and to hurt or be hurt by others. We can see these horizons most clearly in our own behavior, but if we look we see them in others' behavior as well. We see these horizons automatically and implicitly, of course; it is a great help in understanding both our own and others' behavior to have some concepts that can pull these implicit horizons into explicit focus. We shall spell out some of these concepts in Chapter 9. For the time being, we shall be content to list some questions that we must ask. Toward whom is the behavior in question oriented? Often one action in the presence of a number of other people combines a number of messages at once. How does the behavior express a movement or solidify the status quo in the already-existing agreement between the people? There is always already some agreement, even among strangers in an elevator, about what certain behavior will mean and how certain moves will confirm the already existing anonymity whereas certain others will modify it to create sympathy, sexual attraction, competition, and so on.

Having inquired into the temporal, spatial, and interpersonal horizons that control the perceptions and actions of a particular person in a particular situation, we have already made some interpretive judgments about how that individual sees the world and his place in it. We will have had to assume a number of things about his being-in-the-world. The better we know him, the less we have to assume and the more we can say that we "know." All our interpretations will fall into a *pattern* that is a unique variant of our already existing understanding of what it is like to be a person. The goal of our analysis is to see that pattern as clearly as possible. His behavior is our datum; its meaning is our quest. Its pattern is intelligible to us if and only if we can put it all together into the coherent whole of his being-in-the world. Behavior tells us how he *lives* in his world. It reveals to us the structure of his world in his own experience. It makes public what is theoretically private: his experience. It expresses that network of meanings that his world is to him. It is already intelligible to some extent; a phenomenological analysis can make it more so.

In summary, to understand a piece of behavior, first, we must see that behavior in the context of the person's immediate perceptual field. We may analyze that field by describing a number of horizons that his *experience* of the field synthesizes. Second, we must see that field in the context of the person's world: how he construes it and his place in it. The more data that we have, the more personal can our understanding of him become— the more we can know him in his uniqueness. Third, this process of understanding is an articulation of what we already implicitly understand. His behavior speaks to us, and we understand it as his speaking—as an expression of his being-in-the-world. The goal of phenomenological psychology is to open for our understanding as many layers of that expression as we can.

PART
II

METHOD

CHAPTER

3

UNDERSTANDING
AND COMMUNICATING

In considering the methodology of psychological investigation, the most important single fact is that we, the investigators, like those we investigate, are being-in-the-world. We are experiencers, giving meaning and receiving meaning. The processes and structures that we investigate in others' experiences are essentially the same processes and structures that do the investigating.[1] We seek to understand something, which means that we seek to make its meaning clear to ourselves. After we understand something, we seek to communicate what we understand to others. That is the essence of science in its broadest sense.

The methodological question is: How can we make an event reveal itself in its many-layered meaning?[2] In order to reveal the many meanings of an event, we must come to see clearly the experiences of the participants, whose intentions and perceptions *are* the event's meanings. Then we understand. Once the event and its meanings are understood, we want to make them clear to someone else. We must therefore be able to expose our experience so that it can be seen clearly by someone else. In both steps of this process, the same task presents itself. In understanding I want to re-create my daughter's experience in my own, and in communicating I want you to re-create my experience (of her experience) in yours. How can communication be achieved systematically and rigorously?

We know that this process is not impossible, for every day we understand others and communicate with them so that they understand us.

What is difficult is to be systematic and rigorous, to overcome *not* understanding or not communicating, to correct *mis*understanding and *mis*communication. Even though science is an extension of the most natural processes of man, it is not enough for psychology to involve *just* ordinary experiencing. Ordinary experiencing is a miraculous event, and we must build upon it, but it is also subject to error, narrow-mindedness, bias, and preconceptions. Phenomenological psychology is not *just* the use of common sense; it is a refinement of common sense that seeks openness where common sense is closed, discernment of what common sense misses, and clarity where common sense is muddled. But we are certainly stuck, as in using common sense, with experience as the original and final source of our understanding.

When I see my neighbor, Ms. Smith, addressing another person angrily, I do not have to discover methodologically that she is angry. I know it immediately.[3] Further watching, listening, and questioning of Ms. Smith can reveal to me something of why she is angry. She tells me her point of view, how the world looks to her, and how the other whom she was addressing angrily appeared within that world. This recital, too, does not require methodological intervention; it happens spontaneously, and the only thing methodology can add is rigor. Extended acquaintance with Ms. Smith will even enable me to understand how the world design that engendered her anger came to be as it is.

In communicating my understanding of Ms. Smith to you, I tell you about her in the same way that any of us tells another about a third person: how she behaves, what she thinks and feels, and how she sees the world. The more systematic and detailed are her remarks to me and mine to you, the less we must fill in the blanks with guesses, inferences, and generalizations, our own or those of other people.

There are several important methodological clues in this description. First, as an *investigator*, I have to learn how to help her talk, and I must learn how to listen. The re-creation of her experience in mine occurs when she talks and I listen. Second, as a *communicator*, I have to learn how to talk and to help you to listen. The re-creation of my experience in yours occurs when I talk (or write) and you listen (or read). All these processes are elementary; they are the stuff of our ordinary understanding of one another as we more or less successfully achieve it every day. But these processes can be performed well or poorly, systematically or casually, rigorously or with bias.

When I say I *know* something *about* Ms. Smith, I mean that she is present within my field of consciousness. When I say I *know* her, I am saying that my relation to her is structured according to certain socially defined patterns called *knowing*, which are different from fearing, loving, and ignoring. All these patterns, however, are aspects of my being-in-the-world. What we usually call *knowing* is a very specialized part of my being-in-the-world. It occurs within the larger context of my total relation to her, and my total relation to her occurs within the larger context of my and our being-in-the-world.[4]

Because my knowing Ms. Smith has a special and unique context, I cannot communicate to you what I know without also exposing those contexts—my being-in-the-world, my field, and my total relation to her. To divorce what I *know* from its contexts would impoverish and falsify it. It would produce a miscommunication and would lead to misunderstanding. To avoid miscommunication, I would have to let you know also about my loving, fearing, or sympathizing with her. Then what I said about her would be more understandable to you. When we tell another about a third person, we invariably do so in subtle ways: using figures of speech, tones of voice, gestures, and postures. Writing for you to read is never as fully communicative as speaking to you directly. This contextual content is not impossible to handle, but it is usually fairly casual and not explicit. It, too, is the stuff of ordinary understanding and communicating and has to be made rigorous.

Putting this thought another way, my *knowing* Ms. Smith inevitably reflects a certain perspective—mine. I cannot tell you anything about Ms. Smith without simultaneously telling you something about myself and my perspective. In everyday discourse, we understand this point spontaneously, but we do so informally. There is no *telling* that is not motivated, for example, and the motivation is communicated along with the official content. This accompaniment is inevitable; there is no perspective-free knowledge.

One of the truly amazing things about our ordinary experience is that we are able to understand one another's perspectives with so little explicit effort. But, of course, we sometimes misunderstand too, and that is because the perspective has not been made clear by the teller or has not been picked up by the listener.[5] Therefore, a critical part of ordinary understanding and an even more critical part of phenomenological psychology, which seeks to improve on it, is to be able to attend to perspectives and to make them clear to others. The fact that you can transcend the limits of your own perspective and understand mine is the basis of all communication of knowledge and understanding. The more each of us does so, the better able we both are to understand. Those who cannot transcend these limits

are so remarkable that we put them in institutions under the labels "psycho-
pathic" and "mentally retarded."

We have been talking about *talking, telling,* and *listening* as if we were
limiting ourselves to conversation and verbal expression. Although we surely
listen to what a person says, we also listen to what he does not say, and we
"listen" to his gestures, postures, and tones of voice as well. Although we
certainly speak words that express what we mean, we also speak through
what we leave out, by saying things at particular times instead of at other
times, and through our general countenance. Communication is initiated
and understood on many levels at once. It is often helpful, when we want
to find out what some behavior means, to ask the person behaving what he
means by it. But it is not always necessary to ask in order to understand
it, nor is what he says the only thing we understand after talking to him.

Returning again to the example in Chapter 1, I have a perspective on my
daughter's perspective on her self and the world. You have a perspective
on my perspective on my daughter's perspective. It seems that in each of
these links of the chain something must be lost. You do not understand
my daughter's behavior as well as I do because you were not there and
because you have not lived with her as I have. I don't understand my
daughter as well as she does, for, no matter how much time and effort I
put into understanding her, I cannot *be* her, and so I shall never truly capture her experience in my own. This failure is surely a problem; the perspectivity of knowledge, once we appreciate its inevitability, should keep
us humble. Yet, from what I have said, you understand *something* about
her, and you fill in the gaps with your usual ideas about what little girls
are like. And I understand something of her experience that night, even
though she uttered very few sentences during the course of the evening. I
have filled in the gaps with what I have come to know of her by watching
her grow up from the vantage point of being her father. Her mother, who
talks to her somewhat more than I do, has a different vantage point from
mine. And all of us have different vantage points from hers. Considered
in this way, it is a wonder that we understand anything about my daughter
at all.

But I am not locked into my vantage point; I can see my daughter from
her mother's point of view. You are not locked into yours. If you have a
little sister and have come to think that such behavior by five-year-olds just
proves that they are spoiled brats who always get their way, then you will
have to adjust this narrow perspective in reading this book. I adjust mine
by knowing what my wife thinks; my daughter adjusts hers by knowing
what we all think. We share our different perspectives and have come to

have something of a common perspective, or, more precisely stated, our common world becomes more and more common and clear as we talk to one another.[6]

To increase the number of vantage points that I can adopt is a great help in being able to understand. Each vantage point, each set of preestablished ideas about what little girls are like, and each psychological theory pulls some aspects of the event into focus and obscures others. A phenomenological psychologist attempts to see an event in as many different ways as possible, he seeks to make explicit as many different meanings as possible, and he seeks to organize an understanding around the most basic context of meaning there is: being-in-the-world.[7]

There are three general strategies that we can adopt to aid us in the task: the phenomenological reduction, imaginative variation, and interpretation. Let us explain these strategies in terms of a simple example. Suppose that you are standing in a crowd of people leaving a theater and that you hear the following conversation immediately behind you:

Boy: How did you like the movie?

Girl: It was nice; I liked it.

Boy: That's good. . . Last time I took a girl to the movies, she didn't like the movie and had a terrible time.

Girl: Gee, that's too bad.

Boy: Yeah; I guess she thought I was an awful klutz to take her to that movie.

Girl: I don't know. . . . Hmm. . . . You think so?

Boy: She wouldn't even let me kiss her good night.

Girl: Oh. (Pause) You know? I didn't like that movie.

It is perhaps the girl who is the good phenomenologist, although probably not a very rigorous one. As the conversation progresses, the boy's remarks reveal more and more fully the real meaning of his initial question. He is ostensibly inquiring about whether or not the girl liked the movie. As far as the girl knows, that is what he wants to know, and she responds to his initial question in terms of its most obvious meaning. But then she listens to what else he says, and she discovers that his initial question did not mean only what she first thought. He was really asking whether or not she likes him, for it becomes clear that his reason for asking is not a concern for her pleasure but a concern for whether or not he is a klutz in her eyes. A moment later, she discovers that the reason he wants to know whether or not she thinks he is a klutz is because he really wants to ask whether or not she will give him some affection. In light of her new information about the various meanings of the initial question to him, she decides to change her initial answer. She is saying to him, in her last comment, "No, I don't feel affectionate toward you." They are both understanding a good deal more than they are willing to say explicitly.

In order for us to have gotten only this far with the analysis, we have had to listen, think, and interpret phenomenologically. The *phenomenological reduction* is a way of listening. To have thought that the event shows how easily women change their minds or how boys always spoil affection by talking too much is to have missed the point. To have recognized the point, we have had to put aside what Edmund Husserl called "the natural attitude"—preconceptions about what the event meant—and to open ourselves to it as fully as possible. The phenomenological reduction is a conscious, effortful, opening of ourselves to the phenomenon *as a phenomenon.* To say that we want to see it *as a phenomenon* is to say that we want to divorce it from our ideas about women changing their minds or boys talking too much. We want *not* to see this event as an example of this or that theory that we have; we want to see it as a phenomenon in its own right, with its own meaning and structure. Anybody can hear the words that were spoken; to listen for the meanings as they eventually emerged from the event as a whole is to have adopted an attitude of openness to the phenomenon in its inherent meaningfulness. It is to have "bracketed" our responses to separate parts of the conversation and to have let the event emerge as a meaningful whole.[8]

To have recognized the point of the event is also to have practiced *imaginative variation.* That is, there are many ways to have seen the event, and we had to see it from the girl's point of view *and* from the boy's point of view in order to have taken the point at all. Each is a possible horizon— his being-in-the-world as oriented to getting something from her and her being-in-the-world as coming to recognize that fact. It was not clear initially what he was driving at, or even that he was driving at anything. He might have been suggesting that they stay to see the movie again or that they talk about movies they had both seen—or just filling up empty time with small talk so as to avoid an awkward silence while they were waiting to leave the theater. All these possibilities reflect ways of hearing; in our imagination we can vary different horizons until "the point" becomes clear. It is even possible that one or both members of the couple were operating in a space that included you—that they wanted you to hear. Some of these horizons are revealing, and some are not. Imaginative variation is imagining the appearance of the phenomenon against the backdrop of various horizons in an attempt to see what the total phenomenon means.

Our analysis has led to the conclusion that the *point* involved an adolescent seduction motif. This conclusion is an *interpretation*. An interpretation is an articulation of meanings as they emerge in the phenomenon when considered as a phenomenon. An interpretation is as good as the meanings available to the interpreter while he experiences the phenomenon. Every psychological theory is an interpretive scheme: a set of concepts used by observers to make intelligible to themselves what they observe. Some theories are richer in interpretive possibilities than are others, but no theory can escape its own limitations. By seeing a phenomenon in one way, we close ourselves to seeing it in another way.[9]

What distinguishes a phenomenological interpretation is its assumptions, as well as its procedures. First, we assume that the people acting and being acted upon already experience the action as meaningful. Whatever we ourselves may think of the event, in a phenomenological analysis we are obligated to describe it in terms of its meanings for the participants. Second, no act or event ever means simply one thing to its participants. There must therefore be some way to deal with multiple meanings, or layers of meaning, simultaneously. In Chapters 7-9 we shall describe three layers of meaning that are always present in every event that involves people.

This discussion brings us to a problem. To be systematic is essential; there must be some routine that enables one phenomenological investigation to be like another. To interpret all events in terms of the kinds of horizons described at the end of Chapter 2, for example, would supply phenomenological investigation with an orderly procedure to guarantee that nothing critical is being left out. But, if such a procedure were adopted, then we would be forcing the event into already existing categories and denying its unique presence and meaning; such a procedure would close our eyes to the constellation of meanings as they actually become synthesized in our experience. Sometimes one or another horizon absolutely preempts others. The phenomenological reduction becomes important in this context, for it is a procedure designed to return us to experience as it is experienced; it is a posture from which we can capture lived experience as it is lived.

Phenomenological psychology has to produce more systematic than informal and casual interpretations, but it also has to remain open to the event in its unique structure and presence and to avoid pigeon-holing it according to a theory that excludes other perspectives. The phenomenological reduction and imaginative variation are strategies designed to assure us that our interpretation is loyal to the event as it presents itself in our experience. Lived experience, in its full openness, is the criterion of the adequacy of an interpretation. There can be no other.

Finally, there is the task of communicating our interpretation in its perspective. We must keep in mind that in communicating with others, we are always communicating our understanding and that our understanding is always based on a perspective. There are no *facts* that are not viewed through a perspective and an interpretive understanding of what is being described. To make rigorous the process of communication, science has always insisted that the communicator describe not only the event in itself, but also the procedures that have led to a particular interpretation. In a formal psychological study, there is a careful description of the method and also a description of previous work that has suggested the main interpretive categories that underlie the study in the first place. In the traditions of science the matter of perspective is taken seriously.

Unlike the physical sciences, however, psychology deals with meanings, intentions, feelings, and ideas—the stuff of experience, which cannot be quantified without distortion. In the measurement of physical things, I can check my observations against someone else's observations very easily. In the interpretation of behavior, the situation is different. How can I know, when I re-create Ms. Smith's experience in my own, that I am doing so correctly? I cannot know; indeed, I can be more or less certain, since I am not Ms. Smith, that I have not done so completely. But I experience her experiencing something, and what I experience is not necessarily wrong just because it is not complete. Indeed, in my experience I have a perspective on her experience, and that is all I have. We never see the totality of anything, from every point of view at once—not even of physical objects. We always know things from our own perspectives. Even when we know Ms. Smith's perspective, we know it only from our own.[10]

Writing, talking, or otherwise communicating phenomenologically, like the routines of reporting in physical science, must convey not only what is understood but also the perspective from which it is understood. When what is understood is understood only interpretively, as in psychology, the grounds for that interpretation, the contours of meaning in the investigator's experience, must be exposed. The phenomenological reduction, imaginative variation, and interpretation are ways to make the investigator's meanings clear to himself. To describe their operation in the research project itself is to make them clear to the reader or listener. Therefore, phenomenological writing is very strenuous, and every phenomenological analysis is in some sense also a self-analysis. Such is the price (and reward) of rigor.

CHAPTER
4

RESEARCH TECHNIQUES

Any discussion of research techniques in phenomenological psychology must necessarily be open-ended and suggestive, rather than definitive. There are several reasons why. First, phenomenological psychology is in a very early stage of development. Phenomenology as a philosophy is barely half a century old; as a cultural movement, it is even younger and limited largely to Europe. On the American psychological scene, there have been phenomenologists for only a decade or two.[1] Second, unlike other methodologies, phenomenology cannot be reduced to a "cookbook" set of instructions. It is more an approach, an attitude, an investigative posture with a certain set of goals. The range of techniques that may be used to implement this attitude is very broad indeed, and only a few of them have been actually tried. Third, the method used in one research project is not necessarily appropriate in another one. Each project presents its own problems, goals, and contours. Almost by definition, to use the same method on two different problems violates the phenomenological attitude—the attitude that seeks to meet phenomena on their own terms and not to press them into the mold of preconceptions.

The goal of every technique is to help the phenomenon *reveal itself more completely* than it does in ordinary experience. This goal may be stated as to uncover as many meanings as possible and their relations to one another as the phenomenon presents itself in experience. The phrase *reveal itself more completely* means to reveal layers of meaning. In the ordinary appearance of an event, its meanings are there in our experiencing of the appearance, but they are implicit and unclear.

We shall divide our discussion according to three kinds of research problems that a psychologist might seek to understand: interpretation of the single, unique event; interpretation of the single, unique individual; and interpretation of a general or repetitive psychological process. There surely will be other kinds of problems that psychologists can attack phenomenologically—involving an institution, a social group, a personality type, a relationship, and so on. But most of this work remains to be done.[2]

THE SINGLE, UNIQUE EVENT

Naturally, anything can count as an *event*, from a single facial expression that lasts only an instant to the occurrence of Nazism in Germany. This category consists of events each of which happens once, in a certain context of space, time, and personnel, and cannot happen again. Understanding past events may be helpful in understanding similar present ones, but such investigations are not explicitly comparative, for comparison necessarily reduces a phenomenon to its commonalities with other phenomena and fails to reveal its uniqueness.[3] Chapter 1 offers an example of a noncomparative analysis. The girl-boy episode of Chapter 3 is another example. A similar event may take place again, but to investigate that event *in its similarity* to other events requires that we choose the events to which it is similar, which in turn requires a prior analysis of the event *in its uniqueness.*[4]

It is, however, true that analysis of single, unique events can help our understanding of other events. In our analysis of my daughter's behavior, we discovered some horizons and structures that are universal. Furthermore, we found some horizons that are always there under certain circumstances (like childhood) and not others. The logic of this kind of understanding is not the same as that in generalizing from one instance; rather, certain horizons will always be there in human experience, and we discover them everywhere we turn. The notion that there is no human experience that is not embedded in spatial, temporal, and interpersonal contexts is hardly the same as saying, for example, that five-year-olds will always change their minds as my daughter did. The latter is an unwarranted generalization; the former is not.

Every professional psychologist is familiar with at least one similar example of obtaining knowledge. The Committee on Scientific and Professional Ethics and Conduct of the American Psychological Association was charged with the task of articulating principles to guide professional practice ethically (A.P.A., 1967). Some shared "sense of ethics" already existed; the task was to codify it for future reference. The committee's approach was described as "an empirical, inductive, critical-incident, content-analysis approach," which would make possible, on the basis of accumulated experience, "to distill from the original code a set of more general principles" (p. vii). Critical incidents, themselves unique, have structural properties that are universal. The universals will always appear, but only if we allow the incident to unfold fully. This difficult work is not, in principle, methodologically different from the phenomenological investigation of single, unique events.

In confronting a single, unique event with the purpose of understanding it, our first task is to let the phenomenon appear as a phenomenon (the phenomenological reduction). There are two, almost opposite, attitudinal shifts in this kind of observation: *stripping* the event of the meanings with which we initially grasp it and *locating* those meanings as a way of identifying the event as it appears in lived experience. That is, we comprehend an event on many different levels at once. In order to become explicitly aware of the many ways we live the experience of the event, we must systematically go beyond the most obvious meanings, strip them away, so that the other nuances of meaning can come into focus. Such a process is analytic, and, as in any analysis, the separated elements must not be taken by themselves except for the purposes of the analysis. Their real importance must be reckoned in the context of lived experience, which is whole, unitary, and integrated.

If you walk into a classroom before class and see the professor putting an outline of the coming lecture on the blackboard, you grasp that event simultaneously on many levels at once: identifying the room as a classroom and identifying a classroom as having some role in your education, which has some role in your life; identifying the man as a professor, whom you know in a number of contexts—personal, professional, as well as by reputation and by his last lecture; identifying the act as part of his *modus operandi*, as anticipating something everyone expects to happen in a minute or two; identifying the content of his writing as what he has said he would talk about today. All these horizons are part of your lived experience of the event. But there are others. The professor's motions express a certain confidence, a certain casualness about this subject matter that is different from your uncertainty about whether you can make a good grade in this course; his up-and-down movement is a symphony of muscular contraction and relaxation, with a certain tempo and pace that express his attitude toward you, toward his work, toward your puzzlement with this course— an attitude or style that could be yours someday if you want it to be or is beyond your grasp. Others enter the room and display multiple cues to their experience: a puzzled look from a student who missed the last class; another from the student who always looks puzzled; a gesture of "Here we go again" by a friend whose recent argument with this professor has led him to dislike everything the professor does; a girl's taking out a mirror and looking at her teeth—is she casual because she has mastered this course, does not care, or is just acting so that her puzzlement will not show? Together the collective motion in the room changes from disorganized, random, individual movements to an organized and collective group attentiveness, promising that something will happen collectively. You realize that this pattern is a larger part of routine understood by everyone; it is a tradition not only of this university but also of universities everywhere, which are structured by the roles of teacher and learner, speaker and listener—a matrix within which you identify yourself now, remembering how you wanted to be part of it and anticipating not being a part of it as soon as you are graduated or drop out. The sun catches the dust by the window, giving that side of the room a glow, and shafts of light penetrate to the opposite wall; some are caught on the professor's shoulder for an instant, as if he were caught in cross fire. He does not notice them, and the analogy would not be his, for he never thinks in military terms. The sounds of chalk on the blackboard punctuate the other sounds of chairs squeaking, fragments of conversation; the chalk sounds continue as the other sounds die down, announcing the group's collectivizing of itself.

Such is the fabric of lived experience. The temporal, spatial, sociocultural, interpersonal, bodily, and ideational horizons all operate simultaneously to produce the lived experience as you live it. It is all already understood by you, but only implicitly. It is the matrix of your being-in-the-world that is the soil from which your own behavior emerges and has its grounding and meaning. All these horizons are involved in some way with your particular mood, from which you behave in response to this lecture. You are bored, fascinated, puzzled, curious, depressed, and frightened, simultaneously and sequentially, in some kind of experiential order that you remember having been through before and anticipate going through again. This event, like every event we may want to understand, is understandable, in fact, is already understood, though not clearly, rigorously, or explicitly. To take lived experience, even in its most trivial and commonplace form, and to operate on it with phenomenological reduction, imaginative variation, and interpretation is to embark on an exciting adventure, at the conclusion of which we are more conscious, more astutely attuned to life, more understanding of ourselves and others, less constricted by conventions, and less plagued by inexplicable moods.

THE SINGLE, UNIQUE INDIVIDUAL

Interpretation of a single, unique individual may well begin with an analysis of a single, unique experience of that individual. When we come to know a person, we string together our experiences of him and let the various contexts in which we have experienced him fade into oblivion. It is wise, therefore, to punctuate analysis of an individual with analyses of single episodes with him, in order to keep the contextual material clearly in mind. Clinical psychologists do so implicitly if and when they realize that they see their clients only in the very special contexts of their offices— a context that conditions both their clients' and their own experiences. Put another way, although a description of an individual tends to focus on *his* lived experience, it is essential to keep in vivid touch with *our own*, through which we know him.

Many interview techniques have been described in detail. Any of them may become phenomenological, depending upon how we listen to a person. In general, we want to listen for horizons, to see the backdrops that make his experience mean to him what it does. Listening for horizons may be compared to an inference like "To see X this way, he must see Y that way." This format of logical inference is not a bad model of listening for horizons, as long as it keeps close to lived experience and avoids sailing off into a portrait organized around logic instead of around experience, in all its paralogical and downright illogical presence. The organizational anchor of phenomenological listening is always how he is-in-the-world.

If we can see what things *mean* to an individual and why, in terms of his structured experience and style, then we are surely seeing a person in his uniqueness. Again, it is well to note that we do so automatically anyway, but informally and casually. Our task is to be rigorous.

How does he "temporalize"? There is a certain pace, a tempo of his life that slows down and speeds up according to his own interests and desires. He stands in some relation to a future and a past. How does he orient himself in general? in specific instances? backward or forward? Most likely, of course, both. In what pattern?

How does he "spatialize"? What are the texture and structure of his field right now? Where are the pushes and pulls of space? the barriers and challenges? Why do they mean what they do to him? Where does he place himself in relation to things? What things stand out and why?

How does he "corporalize"? Is he comfortable with his body? Does it go different directions from those he wants? Is his posture congruent with what he says, or does he give one message with his words and another with his body? What is the pattern of his bodily messages? What is their content, and to what part of his world are they oriented?

What interpersonal agreements bind him? facilitate him? Is he loyal to them? suspicious of them? lonely without them? How does he move in the matrix of culturally determined agreements in order to strike personal ones with you? with his good friends? with strangers? Why are these agreements important to him?

All these questions can be asked separately, but their answers must be integrated, as the individual integrates them into a coherent style of being-in-the-world. Some questions will reveal more important themes than others; going through the list mechanically is not enough. The answers to the questions fall into a pattern that is him. We want to describe him in his uniqueness.

It is worth noting that these questions can all be asked—and answered—without necessarily speaking with the person we want to understand. Of course, conversation is the best way to find out what we want to know, and it is one means by which we understand our family, friends, and acquaintances. It is not, however, always possible to converse, and so we have to see how watching behavior, reading documents, and so on, can yield understanding as well. Jean Piaget (1954) reports that a child in the first year will follow with his eyes an object that is slowly rotated around him. Up to a certain age, he will keep looking for the object that has passed behind him in the direction in which it disappeared; later he will turn and anticipate its appearance on the other side. Piaget interprets this change in behavior as the child's acquiring of a 360-degree spatial orientation. It is an easy inference to make, from behavior to experience, and we do it every day. Your tightness of brow expresses your doubt, your sagging muscula-ture betrays your fatigue, your constant looking toward the door reveals that you are expecting someone to come in (see Allport and Vernon, 1933).

Now, of course, errors from this kind of inference are common enough, but they are usually discovered, which attests how well we understand after all. In everyday life, these "inferences" are hardly inferences at all in the strict sense. As data of various kinds pile up, they form a pattern that begins to take a shape. Because individuals are consistently patterned in their behavior, as well as in their experience, and because behavioral and experiential patterns are inevitably congruent, the sense we have of another's style or orientation toward the world in his experience, gathered from merely watching his behavior, is very likely to be correct—if we have remained open to the behavioral data as they are given to us and if we refrain from classifying ahead of time what they will indicate about a person.

A GENERAL PSYCHOLOGICAL PROCESS

We shall describe two research projects from the recent literature to exemplify some techniques that can be used to study general psychological processes: a study of anger (Stevick, 1971) and a study of empathy (Lauffer, 1971). In the first study, the investigator interviewed thirty adolscent girls, beginning with: "Try to remember the last time you were angry and tell me anything you can about the situation, about what you felt, did, or said." The tape-recorded interviews were open-ended, nondirective, and aimed at the fullest verbal description possible for the subject. Once transcribed, these interview data were systematically condensed and summarized by the investigator, whose repeated question was "What kind of behavior is anger for you?" A summary description of anger for each subject emerged, which included the situational or field properties of the experience, the bodily response, the behavioral tendency, and the felt purpose of that tendency.[5]

The investigator then followed a routine suggested by P.R. Colaizzi (1973), in order to check the findings from the first procedure. This routine contained six steps. First was consideration of each statement on each protocol with respect to its significance for the description of the experience of anger. Second was to record all relevant statements. The third step was to interpret these statements reflectively to determine their meaning, to list each nonrepetitive meaning expression. Fourth was to relate and cluster expressions of meaning. Fifth was to synthesize the expressions of meaning from all the protocols into a single extensive description of anger. Sixth was to reflect on this fundamental description in order to arrive at the fundamental structure. This procedure obviously requires a great deal of judgment from the investigator at every point. The criterion of such judgments is, and has to be, the lived experience of the investigator, which is as stated before, already an understanding of others' experience, albeit an implicit one. Naturally, the routine does not include foolproof safeguards against bias; that, too, must be adjudicated in the court of lived experience. E. L. Stevick invites us all to compare our lived experiences with the following description.

Anger is the experience of being pulled into the world by an important but unreasonable and unyielding other who prevents my doing, having, or being in relation to something of personal importance.

The body in anger is a wanting-to-burst-forth body, a body caught up in the desire to change the world which will not yield to its demands. This desire to change the world may burst forth actually in observable, non-typical behavior, or it may be lived out as a desire for this type of behavior.

The behavior is a thrusting forward, a behavior often ineffective and directionless, but which is the body's attempt to move the world, and the other.

The other, in anger, is transformed into a depersonalized other, not "my mother, father or friend" but simply the other who stands in the way. In the same way the person of the self is somehow derealized; it is a "not me" who strikes out to realize a "necessary" project. This transformation of the self and of the other or of the relationship is never complete, and insofar as the real world relationship remains present to consciousness alongside the magical, transformed world, behavior retains rationality and restrictions.

Awareness of self breaks into the angry mode and effort begins to extract oneself from this affective mode of presence.

Anger is distinguished from fear by its mobilizing effects on the body's behavior and from impatience and aggravation which have as objects things or less important others, or others preventing less important concerns. It is distinguished from crabby, depressed or hurt moods which refer more to a subjective feeling tone than to a mode of acting in and on the world.[6] (1971, p. 143–44).*

In our second example, M. Lauffer's study (1971) of empathy, the investigator interviewed about twenty college students for from one to two hours each. The interview itself followed a task, in which subjects rank-ordered whom they would most like to help among a series of eight minority-group families who were in some kind of trouble. Each of these families was described in a short paragraph; the subjects ranked them, and the investigator then engaged each subject in conversation about his experience of the task, his reasons for his rankings, and how these reasons were justified in his world of view. The interviews were tape-recorded.

The investigator then listened to each interview many times and tried to articulate an understanding of each subject's world structure. Life-space

*This quote from Stevick is reprinted with permission of the publisher from *Duquesne Studies in Phenomenological Psychology: Volume 1* by A. Giorgi et al. Humanities Press, Inc., New York.

diagrams were drawn, various conceptual tools were applied to discriminating types, and the investigator's own immediate impressions of the subjects were duly noted, including an initial intuitive ranking of the subjects according to how empathic they seemed to be and the kinds of empathy that seemed to appear in the data.

The most remarkable result of the study lay in the nature of the investigator's intuitive grasp of empathy as it became manifest in the sifting of the data. To what was the investigator responding? How do we "know" empathy? How do we somehow know about others, respond to them, and become impressed by them in our ordinary experience? Upon reflection, it became apparent that the critical feature of an empathic person is his ability to experience the points of view of others. This much follows from our everyday definition. However, it was further found that one is relatively able or unable to do so depending upon the structure of his world. Empathic being-in-the-world can be described as multicentered, having other centers of meaning and origins of motivation that are nearly as vivid as one's self. Some people live in a world whose structure is rather like a space with a single lightbulb in the center. All events are visible only in the light from that center, and all else is in shadowed darkness. An empathic person, on the other hand, lives in a space with many light bulbs, each of which illuminates a somewhat different side of every object and each of which provides a possible perspective from which to see a pattern of events.

Stated more precisely, to "see" other people as centers of illumination implies an orientation to them in which their points of view are as legitimate as one's own. Such a "seeing," characteristic of the empathic subject, or such a world design thus implies respect for others and furthermore a living awareness of their capacities to feel pain, anxiety, and so on.

The limitations of the metaphor of light bulbs are obvious, yet it comes close to the structure of the world to which we are all sensitive when we use the term *empathy* in everyday life. Regardless of the term we use, however, Lauffer's study made clear that we are in fact sensitive to that structure of experience in others. And it is not, of course, only psychologists who are sensitive to this structure; everyone is. This structure is the critical "thing" that we "know"; but we do not know that or how we know whenever we find ourselves trusting another person to teach our children or share our troubles.

It is clear that all the techniques described in this chapter are laborious and still leave important questions unanswered.[7] The continuing development of psychology may streamline some of the unwieldiness, but there are clearly no shortcuts for the general procedure described in Chapter 3. Naturally, the adequacy of a method also depends on the original purpose of the investigation. Whenever we want more than the kind of understanding that can be yielded with these techniques, we should perhaps inquire why we want that particular something more and whether or not it is valuable. Such complex value questions will have to be deferred here.

CHAPTER

5

METHODOLOGICAL DEVELOPMENT

We must inquire into the next steps in the development of a phenomenological methodology. Doing psychology phenomenologically is not only a pioneering kind of work in terms of exploring new aspects of psychological subject matter, but also, and more important, it requires considerable inventiveness and skill to evolve methods that are appropriate. To repeat, the goal of every technique is to help the phenomena reveal themselves more completely than they do in ordinary experience. By and large, the phenomenon we seek to understand is the being-in-the-world of people. We have said that our approach to this subject matter may follow an exploration of what things mean to people, which leads us to explore the horizons of meaning and how they are organized in the experience of the person into a coherent world and sense of himself as a part of it. How, in concrete, operational terms, can we achieve our goal?

We shall begin by looking at a study of child-rearing practices in lower-class families and shall criticize it from a phenomenological point of view. Then we shall try to see what could have been done differently in collecting, interpreting, and reporting the data. Finally, we shall try to generalize our suggestions into a strategy more general than this particular study but more specific than the recommendations in Chapter 3.

A CROSS-CULTURAL STUDY

Some of the meaning of any behavior is drawn from a preestablished set of meanings, that is, one's culture. Only by looking specifically for these meanings can we see them clearly. And we must look from two points of view. First, we must see what events *mean to the participants;* some of their meanings will be cultural. When the observer shares the cultural background of the participants (region, religious heritage, social class, race, definitions of the world), then this understanding is less difficult, indeed, automatic, and he need merely make it explicit. When the observer differs in cultural background from the participants, then seeing their meanings is a good deal more difficult but not impossible.

In both instances, however, to see clearly, we must, as observers, also scrutinize *our seeing* itself. That is what the phenomenological reduction, imaginative variation, and interpretation are for. This kind of methodological rigor defines a second way in which we must look for and understand the importance of culture in behavior when we do phenomenological analysis.

In an investigation of family patterns of growing up and raising children in lower social classes, E. Pavenstedt (1965) has described a pattern she calls "disorganized":

> The outstanding characteristic in these homes was that activities were impulse-determined; consistency was totally absent. The mother might stay in bed until noon while the children were also kept in bed or ran around unsupervised. Although families sometimes ate breakfast and dinner together, there was no pattern for anything. The parents often failed to discriminate between the children. A parent, incensed by the behavior of one child, was seen dealing a blow to another child who was closer. Communication by words hardly existed. Directions were indefinite or hung unfinished in mid-air. Reprimands were often high-pitched and angry. . . . As the children outgrew babyhood, the parents differentiated very little between the parent and child role. The parents' needs were as pressing and were as often indulged as were those of the children. There was a strong competition for the attention of helpful adults. (Pavenstedt, 1965, pp. 94–95)

Let us take a look at this observation. The difficulty is not that the description is heavily interpretive or that it is bristling with value judgments that condemn this way of life, for all description is interpretive and inevitably emerges from the particular value perspective of the perceiver. The difficulty in this description is that the interpretation is not rigorous and the role of the perceiver's values in the perception and interpretation appears to be almost completely implicit. This failure to recognize the role of values leads the perceiver to see some things clearly and to obscure others. A phenomenological analysis could definitely improve this study.

"The outstanding characteristic in these homes was that activities were impulse determined. . . ." This characterization emerges from the theoretical categories of "impulse" and "control" ("instinct" and "ego" in Sigmund Freud's terminology). The behavior Pavenstedt saw seemed to her impulsive instead of controlled. The difficulty here is that Pavenstedt takes staying in bed until noon and not supervising the children to be impulsive, as opposed to controlled or patterned, when such behavior is obviously both. Rather than expressing an impulse to stay in bed in an uncontrolled and nonpatterned way, this behavior quite clearly *is* a pattern, controlled and following rules, but the patterns and rules are different from those of the observer. This difference is cultural. The next thought, "consistency was totally absent," is simply wrong. The observer could not see consistency, but the parents and children almost certainly could. We might say that our middle-class patterns are "better" or "healthier" for children; that is a value judgment we can make. But the observer does not see a less healthy pattern; she sees only the absence of pattern—the absence of a middle-class pattern.

"The mother might stay in bed until noon while the children also were kept in bed or ran around unsupervised." This relatively neutral description is less objectionable. We have noted that it ought to lead to a different conclusion from that in Pavenstedt's first sentence, for it describes a *different* pattern and not the *absence* of a pattern. It would not be improved much by a quantitative account of how often she stayed in bed or how many minutes the children were unsupervised unless we think, as I do not, that Pavenstedt grossly distorts the facts. It is, after all, the pattern we are after and how this pattern is experienced by the participants—not behavioral frequencies apart from anyone's experience.

"Although families sometimes ate breakfast or dinner together, there was no pattern for anything." Pavenstedt did not look for a pattern, so she saw none. She looked for what could cause psychopathology, and she found an absence of what she implicitly assumed causes mental health: middle-class patterns. The fact that standards for mental health are also middle-class standards hardly needs to be mentioned, and, though these values may be our values as well, we can see the possibility of cultural imperialism here: These people are not like us, and so they are sick. Not that being impoverished does not cause human suffering; but, applied to cultural groups, Pavenstedt's approach leads us to see only absences and not what is present, to assume that these absences lead to mental sickness, and to feel a moral obligation to change patterns without inquiring into whether or not we may be destroying patterns we cannot see by superimposing our own—all in the name of creating order out of chaos.[1]

"The parents often failed to discriminate between the children. A parent, incensed by the behavior of one child, was seen dealing a blow to another child who was closer." This pair of sentences, first an interpretation of the experiential structure of the parent, followed by a concrete datum, is reasonably stated. Again, a statistical count of how often this behavior happened is not as important as a clear seeing of how the parent sees.

"Communication by means of words hardly existed. Directions were indefinite or hung unfinished in mid-air. Reprimands were often high-pitched and angry. . . ." These sentences also offer important observations, as long as we recognize that the phrase "indefinite or hung unfinished in mid-air" refers to the experience of the person being directed. That is, we can *see* whether or not a parent's directive has been understood by a child by watching the child's face, posture, and behavior. If it "hung in mid-air," we hope the investigator is telling us that it did so *for the child*, a conclusion that an observer can reach. We hope that Pavenstedt is telling us not that *she* did not understand, but that *the child* did not.

"As the children outgrew babyhood, the parents differentiated very little between the parent and child role. The parents' needs were as pressing and as often indulged as were those of the children." Again, the first sentence is the interpretation, and the second reports the supporting data. The sequence from data to a literal reading of the interpretation seems fair in this instance. The data are almost quantitative, but the real meaning of the sentences to the writer and the reader involves not the behavioral frequency but the interpretation of a pattern and what it is like to grow up in such a pattern. Now, it is not clear that the differentiation of the child and adult roles is always a good thing. My point here is not that children are no more vulnerable than adults; they are. But indulging children instead of adults does not lead automatically to mental health.[2] The author does not say what she means. She really seems to mean that the parents' experience was structured around their own needs at the expense of sensitivity to their children's needs. This way of saying it may seem to involve a small difference in vocabulary, but it is probably truer to Pavenstedt's own experience; it describes what is more critical than whether or not parents demand indulgence of their own needs, and it describes what is going on better than the language of child and parent roles—roles that can vary immensely without producing psychopathology.

"There was strong competition for the attention of helpful adults." This sentence describes a complex interpersonal pattern of mutual percep-tions. As long as we recognize that the critical content of the sentence deals with how people *see* one another, then it is a decent summary sen-tence that leads us to see what Pavenstedt saw and probably describes what and how the participants themselves *saw*.

The point of this whole exercise is not to argue that we must cleanse our perceptions of perspectivity: our values and reasons for doing the study. Indeed, that cannot be done; there is no perspective-free knowledge. The point is rather that we can see and write more or less rigorously, and that the phenomenological reduction, imaginative variation, and interpreta-tion offer psychology a route to that rigor that can take us beyond culture-bound folklore.

SOME METHODOLOGICAL IMPROVEMENTS

Pavenstedt's method in her study included interviewing family members, observing them at home, and teaching their children in nursery school. These overt routines should have yielded better results than they did. Talking to people or, rather, listening to them and watching them, however, can be done more or less well. A great deal depends on how we listen and watch—what we listen and watch for. A phenomenological approach to listening and watching aims at understanding events in terms of the mean-ings they already have in their natural setting. Pavenstedt did not have this focus. The events she observed were not allowed to speak for themselves. Pavenstedt should have sought the meanings these events had in their natural setting, in the experience of her subjects. Because she did not explore their experience explicitly, the natural meaning of the events was not clear. She imposed her own culturally imperialistic meanings on the events. She failed to let the events and their already existing meanings in the experience of her subjects reveal themselves.[3] How could she have done better?

Suppose that you are observing a family and you note that the mother stays in bed until noon and that the children run around unsupervised. Your first reaction to this mother's behavior should not be automatically translated into a report that she is impulsive and uncontrolled or that there is no pattern to anything. That is one meaning of the event—perhaps the meaning that any "conscientious" middle-class parent would see. But the most relevant meaning of this event is to be found in the experiences of mother and children: its "natural" meaning in its "natural" setting. How can you go about discerning the natural meaning of the event and what it has to do with the larger picture of who-these-people-think-they-are-in-what-they-think-is-the-world (their being-in-the-world)?

The obvious answer to this question is simply to *ask* the people involved. That is not, however, as easy as it sounds. Pavenstedt surely asked questions and listened to the answers; that is what an interview consists of. Everything hinges on what the question is, how it is asked, how the listening takes place, and what the larger context of the conversation is—diagnosis, examination, exposure, help, investigation, and so on. Psychologists have, from time to time over the decades, taken seriously the task of asking people what they wanted to know from them. Sigmund Freud was a master at this obvious task, and the whole of psychoanalytic theory is based on a program of scrupulously careful listening. Clinical psychologists since Freud have, of course, followed his procedures to some extent or other. Jean Piaget was surely one of our century's most skillful interviewers; he scrupulously asked children why they thought as they did, and he developed our best theory of cognitive development. More recently, Robert Coles (1967, 1971) has had notable success in practicing psychology merely on the basis of sensitive and skillful listening. A. Esterson (1972) also offers us a remarkable demonstration.

Even though we can find such examples, psychologists in general have come to be enormously skeptical of so-called verbal reports, that is, of what people say. Observing behavior has come to be preferred to asking and listening as a methodological technique, and we shall do well to examine the source of this skepticism. Only by overcoming these traditional objections shall we be able to do psychology in this way without falling into the obvious traps that have spoiled, for example, the Pavenstedt study.

The three most common criticisms of asking and listening as research techniques are, first, that what we hear is so riddled with the subjective biases of the individual that it has very little value for the science of psychology; second, that a good deal of what goes into the production of behavior is not conscious and that people do not, as Freud demonstrated, really know their own minds; and third, that what people tell psychologists is more what they think psychologists want to hear than anything else. Let us take up each of these criticisms as part of our quest for a viable methodology.[4]

Unlike the second and third criticisms, the first one dissolves immediately as soon as we recall that it is precisely "subjective biases," that is, how people experience events and what their horizons of meaning are, that we *want* to explore. These "biased" reports *do* have value when we seek the truth about so-called biases.

The second criticism is more instructive. We dealt with the problem of unconscious motivation in Chapter 2, drawing a distinction between implicit and explicit knowledge. We are often not explicitly aware of why we do or see things in particular ways, but we surely "know," in some sense, how to do them, or we would not do them. This observation does not, however, solve the substantive problem of how to bring into explicit awareness, so that it can be reported, that implicit knowledge that so often guides our experience. In fact, the "unconscious," as traditionally understood, is not far removed from those horizonal factors in experience that interest us the most. They are so basically and uncritically assumed by most people that asking about them sometimes barely makes sense. We could not simply ask one of Pavenstedt's mothers, "What horizons of meaning condition your world view and personal identity in such a way that you fail to be sensitive to what I have been trained to be sensitive to in children?" We shall have to return again and again, as our methodology develops, to the issue of how to persuade people to describe aspects of their own experience to which they are unaccustomed to paying attention.

The third criticism is perhaps even more instructive, for people do tell psychologists what they think psychologists want to hear. The entire role structure of psychologist and subject is one of examiner and examined, especially in our culture, and the most honest of us cannot refrain from the temptation to say things that will please "the examiner" or cause him to have a good impression of us. It is not simply a matter of telling the truth. There are always lots of true things we can say about ourselves. Once we have decided not to lie to an examiner, we shall still tell him those things that seem to be of most interest to him.

If, and only if, we can overcome the second and third criticisms shall we be able to progress by the obvious technique of asking people what we want to know from them. Once we have an approach to asking and listening that offers some promise of meeting these criticisms, we may be in a position to broaden our procedures from the interview to other observational strategies.[5]

THE SUBJECT AS CO-RESEARCHER

How does it happen that we understand others every day? We hear and interpret their "verbal reports" of what they are thinking and why, and we stake a good deal of our everyday lives on the soundness of this procedure.

We also expect others to take what we say seriously, and we can usually tell when they do not—and then we feel insulted. I am willing to share what I can of my private experience with those people whom I like, trust, and want to know me. Such relationships are common, but they are very different from that between experimenter and subject—I would have felt differently toward Pavenstedt, who was judging severely according to her concepts of mental health and mental illness. The nature of the relationship between people obviously has a powerful effect on what is heard and what is said.

Pavenstedt would have had a difficult time striking up trusting relationships with her subjects. Across social-class and racial boundaries, it is quite difficult; the relationship between examiner and examined is even more fraught with suspicion and wariness. Because a psychologist does not cease to be a psychologist when he does research, the difficulty of the third criticism seems nearly insurmountable. Skillful researchers have overcome it, however, and the guiding theme of such research relationships has been to make the subject into a co-researcher.[6] This kind of relationship itself may best be discerned by examining it phenomenologically—what are the horizons of meaning embedded in the relationship itself? What is required is a clear agreement on what is being sought, why it is being sought, and what will be done with the information. Such agreements are not aided by written contracts and sometimes not even by verbal contracts. The critical cement of such an agreement is the subtle cues to which we are all sensitive when we converse with others. The only way really to convince someone that you are in good faith is to be in good faith. Doing good psychological research requires a certain skill and an attitude found no more frequently among psychologists than among the general population.[7]

Once a researcher has overcome the most obvious difficulties of the relationship within which data are gathered, he must find a way to evoke descriptions from his co-researcher that will tell him what he wants to know, without telling his co-researcher what to say.[8] What kinds of interaction allow this result?

In mulling this problem over, I have nearly reached the conclusion that what is needed is not the development of research techniques but rather the development of researchers. The next step in the methodological development of phenomenological psychology should perhaps involve not concentration on how to obtain the data but rather how to train researchers to be sensitive, self-critical, truth-seeking people. If a researcher genuinely seeks truth, he will want to know how people actually are and will not merely try to confirm his favorite hypothesis. If a researcher is self-critical, he will be able to examine his own experience, practice imaginative variation, and attend to phenomena as phenomena, suspending his prior beliefs.[9] If a researcher is sensitive, he will hear the horizons of another's perceptions as they are reported to him. This argument leads only to the conclusion that to train researchers is tantamount to teaching them to "be phenomenological" in the sense of the general strategies described in Chapter 3.

But we were hoping to be more specific in this chapter. We have already said that listening for horizons is not unlike asking the logical question "What must be true of the other's being-in-the-world for him to say that to me, just as he did, right now?" Such an inference can be consciously made. But I must also be aware of the fact that the same kind of understanding of my behavior is going on in the mind of the other, though probably not as explicitly or carefully. I cannot ask a mother why she stays in bed until noon and hope to discover the horizons of her world, for she may well hear the question as an accusation, misconstruing my horizons but revealing the horizons of how she understands our relationship right now. This event would tell me that she is not being a co-researcher as much as a testee before a judgmental authority. What kinds of remarks by me will increase her trust? Can I hear the increase if it happens? Can I convince her that I am really interested only in how she sees the world and that I do not intend to judge her? What convinces her, and what does that tell me of how she sees the world?

Once she is enlisted as a co-researcher, even tentatively, I can validate her trust by asking her to explain further when I do not understand, letting her know that I really want to understand. I can describe to her what I think she means and invite her to correct it. I can let her know when I really do understand; I can express my willingness to respect her report as the truth. I can suspend moral judgment; she will know when I do. I can offer some of my own experiences and my understanding of them, asking her to compare them with her experiences and her understanding of them. There is an endless list of concrete moves that I can make, some more helpful than others. What will really count, however, is not only what I say but also who and how I *am,* for she will read it, explicitly or implicitly, in everything I say.[10]

The conclusion of this line of thought is that it is usually possible to persuade people to trust us *if we are in fact trustworthy.* The crucial "technique" that allows us to do viable research in this way is to be a certain kind of person.

Such a methodological development is not likely to seem convincing when it is stated so simply. It is actually a very complex matter. Doing psychological research ought to be every bit as challenging as doing psychotherapy—challenging not only to our ingenuity in designing the collection of data, but also to our capability to evoke trust from those we wish to understand—and then to justify that trust.

The real test of such strategies is not whether or not they sound convincing when stated here. The test is in the work and the results of researchers. We have already mentioned several successful researchers of this kind. The most impressive recent demonstration of this strategy is the work of Jules Henry (1971), an anthropologist who spent the waking hours of about a week with each of six families, then reported what he saw and how he interpreted it.

This study needs no advertisement; it speaks for itself.[11] A few comments on Henry's methodology, however, may clarify the difficult question of how to proceed. First, Henry kept elaborate notes of what the people did, what he did, what they seemed to be feeling, and what he was feeling. Second, he read his own data many times, sifting and sorting according to a variety of perspectives, always critical of his own biases in perceiving and reporting, varying his interpretations, looking at the material from anthropological, philosophical, sociological, psychoanalytic, and other points of view. Third, he allowed each perspective to highlight various aspects of the data until the people he was studying emerged *as people*. Multiple perspectives always create the problem of how to relate the perspectives to one another. For Henry, this problem was solved by the simple fact that the housewife he is describing is not a multiple entity, with anthropological, philosophical, sociological, and psychoanalytic segments. She is one person, coherent and whole; the multiplicity of Henry's perceptions guarantees us a full and rich portrait, but it never is allowed to preempt the coherence of the being-in-the-world of his subject.

If we want to appreciate the difficulties, as well as the possibilities of the general strategies described in Chapter 3, we could not do much better than to benefit from a critical reading of Henry's study.

CHAPTER

6

CLINICAL METHODS

What are the goals of clinical psychology? The assessment and treatment of individuals whose life problems seem overwhelming to them. Such an answer is surely correct according to professional traditions, but it also begs many questions. What is involved in seeing one's life problems as overwhelming? The most obvious answer revolves around that metaphorical verb *seeing*. Life seems intolerable. That one *sees* things in a certain way or lives *seeming* in a certain way has something to do with experiencing. All the concepts discussed in Parts I and III elaborate what is involved in experiencing.

We may therefore restate the goals of clinical psychology more precisely. The assessment procedure is one in which an individual can come to see more clearly how he sees things, how the world seems to him. The treatment procedure is one in which a person can find alternative ways of seeing things, of interpreting the world, and of being-in-the-world.[1]

MARIE, A DISTRAUGHT WOMAN

Suppose that Marie, a twenty-year-old woman, appears at the office of a clinical psychologist seeking help for a personal problem that seems to her to be insurmountable. She reports that she has been dating a fellow student, Jim, for several months, that she has fallen in love with him, and he with her, but that now she is obsessed with the idea that he is in love

with someone else or seeing other women. She believes him when he re-
assures her, but her suspicion keeps returning, and she has begun to spy on
him and never seems to cease needing his expressions of loyalty, which she
demands more and more. Jim is becoming impatient with her; she knows
she is being irrational but cannot seem to settle for things as they are. When
pressed for how she wants things different, she can only say that she wants
to "be sure of him," even though she knows she has no reasonable cause
not to be as sure as the situation warrants.

If you were the clinical psychologist from whom Marie is seeking help,
what would, or should, you do? The first and central task is to understand
her and to help her understand herself. In terms of our statement of the
goals of clinical psychology, it is to help her to see more clearly just how
she is seeing the world and what options there are for seeing, and for being
in, the world.

In this chapter, we shall describe briefly some clinical approaches that
are appropriate to these goals and how they may be helpful to Marie. Then
we shall take up psychological assessment.

THEORIES OF PSYCHOTHERAPY

Carl Rogers (1942, 1961) makes specific recommendations for creating
the optimum therapeutic field, and he does so on the basis of his understanding of personality in general. Let us first describe his understanding
of personality, which emerged from therapeutic work with individuals and
from observing this process with something like a phenomenological attitude.

According to Rogers, the most important things about a person are
unique to him. Two people may perform what seem from the outside to
be similar or identical actions, but the most important aspect of any action
is what it means to the individual. The meaning of events initiated or
endured must be reckoned from the point of view of the person initiating
or enduring them. The loss of a lover thus does not mean the same thing
to everyone who endures it, and any rebellious action that may follow does
not mean the same thing to everyone who responds in this way. The center
of meaning resides within each one of us,[2] and, if I am to understand you,
I must know what your losses have meant to you and what your rebellions
have meant to you.

According to Rogers' concepts (1951), the individual's own experiential
world forms one system, and his organism forms another system; psychopathology results when the two systems work at cross purposes. If, for

example, my rebellious behavior after the loss of a lover means to me only that I am seeking what I want and deserve, I am deceiving myself by excluding organismic, bodily anger from my interpretation of myself. There are many occasions on which we have a vested interest in not facing something we really feel. It is therefore easy to see the wide applicability of Rogers' way of understanding a person with problems.

The therapeutic task is to bring implicit meanings, like our feeling angry, into explicit awareness. The most significant achievement in therapy, according to Rogers, is therefore self-acceptance. Inherent in all personal problems is a rejection of a part of ourselves that is too real to be ignored but too unacceptable to be admitted—unacceptable because we are all busy maintaining our *concepts* of ourselves.[3]

Rogers' recommendations to therapists are all designed to create a situation in which self-acceptance can take place. The first requirement is for the therapist to accept the patient unconditionally. This acceptance creates a field in which the client feels both understood and accepted. Many of our usual life situations are such that we are accepted, but we fear that we would not be if we were really understood. Or they are such that we are understood and therefore not accepted (by parents, teachers, friends). Rogers' therepeutic field, in its texture and structure, seems to invite display of the very worst we have to offer, thus testing our notion that we are not really acceptable as we are. The atmosphere is one of trust, confidence, warmth, and assurance, supported by the unconditional regard of the therapist.

In the example of Marie, Rogers would seek to understand the unique features of how she sees the world and herself in it. He would not suppose that "jealousy" is always the same thing but would rather follow the pattern of meanings that characterize Marie's unique experience. He would, however, suppose that Marie was having other feelings as well, which might engage her organismic system but have no place in her current concept of herself. For example, Marie may well be "depressed," very guilty, and down on herself—in the sense that her bodily responses frequently mimic those of her mother when her father abandoned the family years ago. Although her mother became manifestly "depressed" and blamed herself for her husband's leaving, Marie has always seen herself as cheerful and self-confident. She is therefore not able to imagine herself as like her mother in the least, though she *is* somewhat like her and has been ever since her father left.

The feelings that Marie has about herself, like her fear that she will not be able to sustain a relationship with a man, are also feelings that she cannot admit to herself. These "feelings" are not only "inside" Marie; they permeate the way she sees and relates to the world. But her explicit perceptions of herself and of Jim do not permit such "unacceptable" meanings to be clear, for she is bent on not being like her mother. She is therefore *closed* to important aspects of her own experience. She is terrified that what happened to her mother will happen to her, but what she does not appre-ciate is that she is really like her mother and, on a level of experience that is unclear to her, that she knows that she is. Her feelings of being unworthy of love, of deserving to be abandoned, of failing where she thinks her mother failed are hidden from her explicit understanding of herself and of the world, but they are there nevertheless, embedded in every perception of Jim as he happens to glance at another woman.

Rogers' therapy would provide an interpersonal arena in which Marie need no longer maintain her *concept* of herself as cheerful, self-confident, and utterly unlike her mother. Facilitated by Rogers' unconditional positive regard, she could come to explore her perceptions of Jim, herself, and her mother—knowing that her relationship with Rogers at least will not collapse if she opens herself more fully to her own experience. She may even come to understand her mother better, to accept that her mother's life is not a total failure, to see that her being like her mother is not a complete tragedy, and to understand that her perception of Jim engages horizons of meaning that she need not be frightened of nor believe in totally. Most of all, she will come to accept her feelings of unworthiness simply as feelings that she has, not as aspects of herself to be ashamed of or as signs that she *is* unworthy.

According to George Kelly (1955), as well as to Rogers, it is the individual's own point of view that counts. But Kelly has devised a different theory with which to understand that point of view. A *construct* is a category of meaning by means of which we *construe* ourselves and the world. A person's constructs are organized through his attempts to understand and control his world, and that organization is his personal map of the world. The essence of therapy, according to Kelly, is to reveal alternative ways of construing the world. This process opens up options for movement within one's space that have been concealed by the way the individual sees things.

The best way to understand what Kelly means by a *construct* is to look at his ingenious way of assessing an individual's constructs. Suppose that I give you three items, a bicycle, a motor cycle, and an automobile, and that I ask you to classify two as alike and different from the third. You could use such criteria as having two wheels, being power-driven, and being owned by my family to complete the task. You may have no preference among three possible groupings. If, however, I ask you to list the six most important people in your life and then to perform the same task just once for each possible group of three in that six, I will have a good idea of the salient categories of meaning (constructs) that control your construing of your social space. Furthermore, although the task looks very intellectual, the emotional flavor of our lived experience will come into play just as it does in our everyday construing of the world.

Suppose that Marie were to go through the exercise of classifying two alike and different from the third in each possible combination of three among just four people: her father, her mother, her boyfriend, and herself. The results might well be something like those in the following chart.

mother father Jim	mother father	Jim
mother father self	mother father	self
father Jim self	Jim self	father
mother Jim self	Jim self	mother

What she would have done here is to use the single criterion of age in every instance, and the task has been performed very mechanically and without subtlety. Kelly would understand that this approach to the task is, in one sense, simply obvious but, in another sense, far from representative of how Marie sees people. A second performance of the task might be based on the mechanical criterion of gender. If Marie were to do the task mechanically again, he would ask her to do it yet a third time, not necessarily with different results but using different criteria. What criteria would she choose? Eventually she would run out of superficial criteria like height, weight, and complexion—if she insisted on using them—and would have to bring into focus aspects of the individual's appearance to her and of what they mean to her, which are more horizonal and less focal. For example, she might classify her father and Jim as alike and different from her mother on the basis of what she would call "independence." What does "independence" mean to her, and why do people have this meaning? Who else has this meaning? Does she see herself as independent?

The effect of this exercise is clearly to open Marie to an explicit awareness of horizons of meaning that, though implicit, are running her life and repetitively constricting how she construes the world. Criteria like "they don't like me," or "they make me nervous" will emerge as salient aspects of how she perceives important people and as crucial dimensions of her experiential life. The order and pattern of her experiential life and of her interpersonal behavior will come into vivid focus, and she will learn what she already knows but does not know that she knows. She will learn *how* she knows what she thinks she knows, and she will see it as embedded in her perceptual style.

The whole point of Kelly's exercise is finally to make clear that there are alternative ways to perceive people—indeed to construe the world and thus to structure that space among people within which we live and move every day. It may have been easy to say to Marie that she need not see her boyfriend as she sees her father, but simply saying it would have had little effect. It is like telling someone who is depressed that he need not be depressed. But, when this perception is revealed as a part of a pattern, *Marie's* pattern, her perceptual and experiential world, and when she sees what and how she sees, then this choice of how to see her boyfriend is a very different matter. We have here almost a routine that can teach the phenomenological-reduction and imaginative-variation (Chapter 4) techniques for seeing more clearly what and how and why we see as we do.

The structure of our lived world involves a great deal more than interpersonal constructs. A fuller analysis of one's world is contained in the psychology of Ludwig Binswanger (1953, 1958b, 1963). The basic forms of human existence are described by Binswanger in terms of three differently structured worlds, or landscapes, that supply the horizons for our being people at all: the world of the air, the world underneath the ground, and the world upon the surface of the earth. We would not say that these worlds are *known* to us; they form the structural context within which our knowing (or feeling, acting, or being) takes place. They are horizons.

The world of the air is a definite landscape in which we sometimes totally *are* and always partly *are*. *Possibilities* abound. Limits are absent. Time is racing, fleeing rapidly into the future, zipping ahead into glorious images of what could be. Idealism is reality. The bodily sense of flying as a bird flies, free of earthly restrictions, of exhilaration and boundless energy, combined with a mood of unbridled optimism and the cognition of utopian fantasy, together produce a world in which our being in the world soars with the creativity and spontaneity of life itself.

The structure of the world under the earth, which underlies a different form of being in the world, is one of *necessities*. Time passes steadily and relentlessly, and the passage of time leads only to getting older, draining of vitality, rotting, rusting, or decaying away into the inert stuff of sheer matter. One's self is heavy, like a body in its ponderous, weighty, substantial intransigence. The mood is one of pessimism. The darkness of the grave, the dampness of the tomb, the smothering closing in of being beneath the earth—with no room, no space, no freedom, no movement—characterize this world. We are trapped, and escape from the confinements of necessity is impossible. The only change time brings is progressive deterioration from within and crushing by inexorable weight from without.

These two worlds are the worlds of each of us when we are in certain moods. But what is a mood? Experientially, a mood is not a physiological state of affairs; it is a way of being-in-the-world.

The world of standing, or striding, on the surface of the earth is the world of practical action. We all must somehow reconcile the flight of imagination in the realm of the possible with the limits of human finitude and the realm of the necessary. In the world on the surface of the earth, we take up the possible and temper it with the necessary, and we take up the necessary and vitalize it with the possible. Human being in the world transforms both: I shall die some day, but today I am alive; today I am alive, but I shall die some day; my love for you is boundless, but I must also spend time doing the work of the world; I must spend time doing the work of the world, but that work and that world are rendered meaningful by my boundless love for you. In his analysis of Ellen West, Binswanger demonstrates that these three basic forms of human existence have a concrete presence in the experiential world of all of us.

Returning again to the example of Marie, we see that Binswanger's approach is not a technique for unveiling implicit horizons of experience; rather it is a theory of which horizons are universally present in human experience. It is a philosophy of man, of moods, and of therapy. It implies that the existential situation is one of possibilities within a framework of necessities, of options within limits. At any given moment, the possibilities may be all that is apparent, whereas, at another moment, only the necessities may appear—depending upon our mood. But moods are landscapes, whole worlds, which, in their extreme forms, close off possibilities or necessities, leaving the other as everything. To regain the perspective of possibilities *within* a framework of necessities is neither to soar in the free air nor to decay under the soil; it is to be a human being, true to the existential situation in which both soaring and decaying are facts of life. Marie does have some control over her life, most notably over herself, but she does not have total control over things that have happened to her or may happen to her. Neither her dream of total security with Jim nor her nightmare of the inevitability of his betrayal is the whole story. Furthermore, the future with Jim is not all that is at stake. Her entire being and her entire world are expressed in this problematic relationship. Binswanger generalizes from Kelly's "others" to the "world."

There are, of course, many other phenomenological or near-phenomenological ways to do psychotherapy.[4] A. Barton (1974), however, has used phenomenology neither as a technique, a goal, nor a philosophy of therapy, but as a research tool. In describing the space, the time, and the agreements that actually occur in the therapies of Freud, Carl Jung, and Carl Rogers, Barton has shown that every therapist has a theory and that this theory operates in certain crucial ways in every psychotherapy. It structures the therapist's gestures and postures, marking off the possibilities and the necessities of the therapeutic relationship—and ultimately of life. And it offers an order where the patient initially experiences disorder. The "theory" here is not just a collection of articulated propositions, though they are important; the "theory" is *lived* by the therapist, and ultimately by the patient, as a vision of life and truth that can make seemingly insoluble problems comprehensible and tractable.

Because both patient and therapist are often unaware of what Barton calls "the transformative power-of-having-a-theory," they tend, in the heat of therapeutic action, to neglect the fact that the "reality" to which they are now so acutely attuned is a matter of perspective and not "objective." A phenomenological study like that of Barton reveals what the "natural attitude" of most therapists and patients cannot reveal—that there are many viable visions of life and truth in our culture that can improve upon the one the patient initially brings to therapy. The crucial helpfulness of all therapies is in helping the patient to find one viable approach, not to arrive at the "objective truth" about human relations and behavior.

Put another way, phenomenology enabled Barton to adopt an attitude (the phenomenological reduction) that in turn enabled him to see psychotherapy more clearly than it is seen with the natural attitude. That is, most therapists are committed to particular theories, visions of life and truth, and styles of taking up the exigencies of living and facing what must be faced. This commitment is not a bad thing—indeed it is a crucial part of the therapy itself. But it does lead the therapist to assume that *his* version of reality is what is "really real." This assumption is exactly what Edmund Husserl meant by "the natural attitude."

For Marie to look at *how* she looks at the world and for Barton to look at how therapists look at the world, is, in both instances, to adopt a special perspective in order to scrutinize everyday experiential life. The special perspective is "the phenomenological reduction"; and our everyday experiential life is conducted with "the natural attitude." Barton is, in essence, trying to do for psychotherapists what they try to do for their clients: to make clear the horizons of meaning that are embedded in everyday experience. Naturally, in either working with patients or with therapists, the phenomenologist is faced with a difficult task. The only reason for attempting it at all lies in the conviction that the horizons of meaning in a person's experience contain the crucial factors we must understand if we are to understand human behavior.

At the same time, however, phenomenology is, in another sense, also a theory, a vision, and a style. What makes phenomenology different is its consciousness of the transformative power, and hence the central role, of theory, vision, and style. It understands none of these factors as propositions about objective truth. It is keyed to the way in which these three become *lived,* by both patient and therapist, and it appreciates that this change in how one *is*-in-the-world is the essence of psychotherapy.

Phenomenology, as a therapeutic style, also seeks to *apply* this insight, of the central role of theory, vision, and style, directly and specifically to everyday life—what Rogers, Kelly, and Binswanger would all try to do for Marie. This focus on the being-in-the-world of the patient, as it is lived by him everyday, steers a course away from the more specialized visions of other therapies and tries to work with precisely who and how the patient himself *is.* It also encourages the patient, quite explicitly, to focus on that same crucial nexus of how he is every day rather than directing his attention toward the provocative, but esoteric, "realities" of traditional therapies.

PSYCHOLOGICAL ASSESSMENT

What kind of understanding could emerge if Marie were advised by her doctor to submit herself to what she thinks must be the X-ray vision of a psychologist? C. T. Fischer (1971) has compared such a situation with a phenomenology of the invasion of privacy and has concluded that this routine may well produce a fearful and defensive, if not angry and insulted, posture in Marie. Such a posture, then, is all too often taken for the expected signs of psychopathology. Perhaps psychological testing is a self-fulfilling prophecy; perhaps it is a bad idea in the first place.

If, however, we keep in mind that assessment is really an attempt to clarify what things mean to a person, then the routine need not be one of *submitting* to evaluation. It can be an opportunity to learn something about how one views the world, together with a person who has some helpful skills in bringing people's points of view into focus. There are, therefore, certain kinds of things the psychologist might do to transform a threatening situation into a *cooperative* one, in which both the psychologist and the client have the common goal of understanding the client better. Fischer (1970) suggests, first, that the individual being assessed and the psychologist ought to agree ahead of time on why they are both there, what they want to draw from the experience, and how they will proceed; second, that the psychologist ought to explain his impressions and invite the client to comment on them, modify them, expand them, and relate them to what he thinks is important; third, that the psychologist ought to write his report in language the client can understand, then ask the client to read the report, dictate his reactions, and explain his view of these important matters—these contributions to be appended to the written report or, even better, made an integral part of it; and fourth, that the person who is assessed should be the sole judge of who should read the report.

This approach to psychological assessment not only assures the person that his legal and moral rights will be respected; it also takes his lived experience seriously enough to make it the court of adjudication on any disagreements.[5] It brings into focus the meanings of events, both in the test materials and in the person's everyday world, and how they are organized into his total being-in-the-world.

A PHENOMENOLOGICAL CLINICAL PSYCHOLOGY

After our brief look at psychotherapy and assessment, let us try to clarify, in terms of the present book, some ideas about phenomenological clinical psychology in general. We said in Chapter 4 that *listening for horizons* is a crucial part of understanding an individual person. This strategy was described as something the investigator can do, and it was likened to the process of logical inference. In our present discussion of clinical psychology, it becomes clear, first, that it is also something the client can learn to do for himself, and, second, that for him to do so does not involve anything like an inference but rather is an opening of himself to his own lived experience.

The critical goals of clinical psychology can be achieved by helping people to come into vivid touch with their lived experience.[6] How can clinical psychology go about helping people do so? Rogers' careful structuring of the therapeutic field in such a way as to produce self-acceptance is a helpful approach. Kelly's systematic laying out of the operative interpersonal constructs is another. Binswanger's attempt to bring into focus those landscapes of lived experience that are universal offers yet another way to help the client to listen for the horizons of his own experience. In Fischer's approach to assessment, the individual being assessed learns as much about his lived experience as the psychologist does. We may also say that a systematic exploration of the physiognomy of the field, of oneself in time and time in oneself, and of interpersonal agreements (Chapters 7-9) may be an approach to our task. All these clinical techniques are designed to open the individual to his experience as he experiences it.

PART
III

SOME UNIVERSAL HORIZONS

CHAPTER
7

THE PHYSIOGNOMY
OF THE FIELD

Behavior must always be understood in the context of the perceptual field within which it occurs. A perceptual field, we recall, must be described in terms of lived experience, for it is lived experience that, by structuring itself, integrates all the meanings that we are interested in. We may analyze an experiential field into horizons and horizons of horizons, as we did in Chapter 1, and we may put it into a larger context of being-in-the-world, as was noted in Chapter 2. But a field has its own level of organization. That organization can best be approached through description of the field's physiognomy.[1]

The physiognomy of a field is a powerful part of our experience. We can easily notice it in our own experience, and, with some practice, we can also "see" it in the experience of another.[2] Suppose that you walk into an auditorium. You will notice the rows of seats in a kind of order that is centered on the stage. The décor consists of lines and a demarcation of space such that we are "drawn toward" the podium on the platform. If the auditorium is empty, it will have a feel of ghost town to it.

An auditorium is quite different physiognomically when it is full of people who are eagerly awaiting the arrival of a famous speaker. There is still something missing, perhaps, but the eerie, ghostly atmosphere is gone. When it is full, the auditorium promises an immediate future that we expect. When it is empty, it takes on a timeless quality that gives the experience an uncanny flavor. The full, expectant atmosphere is yet different from that of the same room immediately *after* the speech, when everyone is filing out. Such a perceptual field has a movement that negates the directionality force of the room itself, which pulls us toward the stage. Of course, the movement is understandable to us by virtue of the temporal experience of "having heard the speech," and that temporal dimension prevents the two contradictory vectors of the physiognomy from being an anomaly. If we arrive at 8:00 P.M., thinking the speech is to begin then, only to discover everyone coming out (because it actually began at 7:00 P.M.), our physiognomic perception is anomalous. Our temporal horizon of expectation does not allow the exiting movement to make sense immediately.

These experiences, and hundreds like them every day, demonstrate how temporal, spatial, and interpersonal horizons are synthesized into the physiognomy of a field. But these particular experiences are only examples. They are probably shared by all of us to some extent, and so they do not tell us how different people experience different physiognomies, even in the same room. For some people, every room is an auditorium where everyone else is oriented toward them on the stage. For others, a room full of people is not a stage until something happens that makes it become one. Such a shift in physiognomy occurs when we fall down at a stand-up party, for example, or when the chairman of a meeting suddenly asks us to comment on the group's problem of the moment. Some of us arrange things in order to make such shifts happen. We may respond to the physiognomy by being chronically embarrassed or self-conscious or by being stage-struck and exhibitionistic. The differences between your and my physiognomic fields and between what you and I may *do* to manipulate them depends on the larger structure of our experience and orientation to the world. For some of us, every social situation is a platform, for others, an embarrassment. We structure our fields in ways that are characteristic of us personally. We do so in our experience—by seeing situations in such and such a way. And we do so in our behavior—by shaping situations into such and such, into which we then place ourselves behaviorally.[3]

ABSTRACT AND CONCRETE SPACE

Let us think about the physiognomy of the field of a handball court, a tennis court, or a ping-pong table. Such a perceptual-behavioral field requires instantaneous reactions, and so our understanding of the structure of the space is likely to be "in our bones," or in our muscles, in our bodies. We can feel in our bodies when space pulls us here or there. Very often we respond to perceptual cues, like the movements of our opponent, without thinking about possibilities in any systematic way. This tendency enables a clever opponent to mislead us with his movement, to fake one thing and then do another, and thus to draw us out of position. Playing against a deceptive opponent, we learn to ignore his fakes and to avoid responding prematurely. Such learning involves a transformation of our perceptual field from a *concrete* spatial structure set up by his preliminary movements to an *abstract* one of possibilities—until he has committed himself by hitting the ball. When his preliminary movements indicate that he will hit the ball to one place, that place pulls us, and we move toward it. The pull toward that preferred part of the court is the structure set up by our perception of his preliminary movements. After we have learned to ignore the preliminary movements, the entire court remains a space of equal possibilities, a hypothetical space that becomes actual only when he has committed himself by hitting the ball.

The distinction between *abstract* and *concrete* spaces is a very important one in understanding the physiognomy of a field and its role in our behavior. Years ago a brain-damaged neurological patient by the name of Schneider was made famous by A. Gelb and K. Goldstein (1931), who published an extensive analysis of his behavior. Schneider demonstrated a certain kind of spatial comprehension: He was able to slap a mosquito on his left arm with his right hand. This very concrete act demonstrated an understanding of a concrete field of movement that was also present in his ability to pick up a ringing telephone if it was present in his visual field and to grasp tools correctly. Gelb and Goldstein called this kind of behavior *Greifen*, grasping, which is a bodily appropriation of space in very concrete terms. In contrast, Schneider was unable to point *to* his left arm with his right forefinger when instructed to do so. Such behavior, *Zeigen*, or pointing, occurs in a different experiential space from the concrete bodily space of grasping. To point requires construction of an abstract, three-dimensional space in which there are left and right, arms and fingers, and the following of that abstract map in matching motor behavior to instructions. The space of pointing is not lived by us in the bodily sense in which we experience a tennis court or concretely grasp meaningful objects like tools. Similarly, Schneider was unable to go through the hypothetical motions of picking up a telephone or pantomiming the use of tools when they were not concretely present. Such skills require formulation of hypothetical space not marked out by visually present objects and not in fact subject to physical grasping. Compare the experience of absentminded, concrete acts like scratching an itch and pointing to your left nostril with your right fifth finger, and you will see the difference between *Greifen* and *Zeigen.*

Abstract space is the space of possibility. In imagination I can construct possibilities not currently actual, but in order to do that I must abstract from the concrete visual field or situation certain constant principles or regularities that define the limits within which there can be variation, and then I must imagine a variation that is not concretely present. Concrete space, in contrast, is limited to actualities. I can grasp an actual telephone, but not a possible telephone, as long as my space remains concrete. For there is no "possible telephone" in concrete space; only those objects to which I can orient myself in both bodily and motor terms *are* in a concrete space.

In playing handball or tennis, we require instantaneous reactions. But, to play these games successfully, we must go beyond the concrete space given physiognomically and maintain the entire court as a field of possibilities until our opponents have really committed themselves by hitting the ball. Otherwise we shall be taken in by their preliminary movements, fakes, gestures, and postures designed to deceive us. Schneider would probably have been a terrible tennis player, for his ability to sustain a hypothetical space in the face of the sensory cues that make up a physiognomic field was impaired by his brain damage. *Possibilities* were not apparent to him; only actualities were. Possibilities require hypothetical space, abstract space, a conceptualization of the field that can override the immediate, concrete, and physiognomic space of a perceptual-behavioral field.

The distinction between abstract and concrete space is also helpful in understanding optical illusions. In the Müller-Lyer illusion, two horizontal lines of equal length appear to be of different lengths (see Figure 8). We may measure the lines and come to *know*, conceptually, that they are the same length. Yet they continue to *appear*, physiognomically, different.

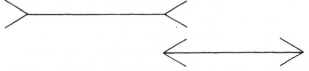

Figure 8. The Müller-Lyer Illusion.

When we say that the Müller-Lyer figures offer an *illusion*, we mean that appearing and knowing fail to match. The *apparent* difference is one experience of the figures; it "places" them in the physiognomic space of things as they appear to us. The *known* sameness is another experience of the figures; it "places" them in the abstract space of linear measurement. Both *knowing* the world and letting it *appear* are ways of orienting ourselves to the world. Some of us are very suspicious of appearances and try to know as much as we can before becoming involved in things. Others of us believe that knowing is less valuable than being able to appreciate appearances. Still others try to use appearances systematically in order to know, to use knowledge in order to see appearances, and so on. Everyone has a style that is characteristic of him personally. One of the differences among people is how they juggle what they know with what appears.

Object constancy is another, similar problem. I see a car as the same size throughout its approach toward me, even though the image of the car grows larger as it comes nearer. In this instance, we have all learned to avoid the physiognomic appearance and to live pretty much by what we know. That is, we know conceptually that the car does not grow larger as it approaches, even though it does so physiognomically.[5] The same physiognomic phenomenon returns strongly, however, when we look from the top of a twenty-five-story building, from which cars appear to us as toys. This return suggests that sometimes our field is structured by abstract spatial coordinates (we *know* that the car is the same measured size) and that sometimes it is structured physiognomically (even though we know that the lines are the same length, they continue to *appear* different).

The categories *abstract* and *concrete* are also applicable to our experience of time. A boring lecture makes a "longer" hour than an exciting one—physiognomically. We make plans according to mathematically conceived hours and weeks, all of which exist in a future not yet here. *Abstractly*, time is a line; *now* is a point on that line. We move along the line ineluctably; the past is forever gone, the future not yet here. Concretely, our experience bounces around from memory to anticipation, the "present" being neither a point on a line nor movement in a single direction but a rich conglomeration of past and future. Even though we may, in imagination, occupy the past or the future, we know we are only in the present. We may experience a memory concretely just as we may experience the car growing bigger as it approaches us, but we are also oriented to what we know abstractly—that the memory is behind us and that the car is the same size.

The interaction between these two kinds of fields in our perceptual experience is not a simple one. It is not always an advantage to live what we know abstractly, rather than what appears concretely. Nor is it really possible to live only according to what we know abstractly, for what we know abstractly is always abstracted from what appears concretely. Indeed, abstract conceptual knowledge always refers to concrete experience, or else it has no meaning. The meaning of what we know is always grounded in concrete fields of our experience, which in turn are organized into the world toward which we are oriented. The equation $2 + 2 = 4$ is a meaningless abstract statement until it refers to something lived by us personally.[6]

THE RETURN TO LIVED EXPERIENCE

We could surely puzzle a good deal over the relation between abstract and concrete spaces, and we could try to formulate in conceptual terms how they influence each other and so on.[7] It is important to see that, although this problem may be interesting theoretically, it may also be somewhat artificial. The solution is amazingly simple and can only be achieved by giving up the conceptual puzzle and returning to the data—the data of lived experience. Lived experience is neither abstract nor concrete; it is both simultaneously, already integrated for us. Our concepts "abstract" and "concrete" are themselves abstractions. To ask how they are related is to pretend that they are separate phenomena. There really is no problem of a "relationship," for their separation is analytical in the first place—useful for some purposes but not characteristic of most experience as it is lived by us in everyday life.

The physiognomic space we must focus on is therefore the lived space that presents itself in our lived experience. The *field* of which we speak must be properly appreciated for what it is, not divided up according to our theoretical notions. We are tempted to understand the field as a display or spectacle. Such a view of the field is not the one we enjoy in lived experience. Being in the world is not a process of passive observation; it is acting and enacting ourselves. The fields we want to examine are not like what we see on a television screen; they are open space, and we are out in it. It surrounds us. A field, as known through lived experience is a space in which we move, manipulate, grasp things, turn them, move around them. We know what we know of the field because of our participation in it. We know according to our purposes, our purposeful movement, and operations upon it. Our relation to the field is more than visual. It is also more than tactile or auditory. These aspects are all synthesized by us as people doing things. The field presents itself as possibilities that are reckoned by us according to our purposes. The field is first of all behavioral *and* experiential.[8]

Much of our behavior is'surrounded by prior plans and ·reflections after the fact. These cognitive acts are surely an important source of meanings for our behavior. But plans and reflections are abstract. They involve consideration of possibilities, future and past. Behavior is that moment in our experience when we articulate abstractions in a concrete presence. Unlike plans, which can be hypothetical, behavior is actual. It fixes an event, in the ineluctable passage of time, with concrete permanence and finality. It is often public and becomes "objective," there for others to see. To behave, unlike the abstract activities of planning and reflecting, is to make an irrevocable commitment.

Let us return to my daughter's episode described in Chapter 1 to see what these conclusions imply. It is possible to puzzle over the relation between her abstract understanding of the space between two houses and its visual presence to her. But neither the abstract nor the visual space is the space she was in. Her lived space had both geometric and visual aspects that we can look at one at a time, but in *her* experience there was no problem in relating them. The physiognomy of her field at the time, which we want to be able to "see" or "understand," was primarily *behavioral.* She was *in* our house, feeling the pull toward the door. The meaning of the door down the hall, standing ajar, was not geometric, nor was it an interesting visual pattern that caught her attention. The meaning of the door was based on her intended act of going through it to reach her friend's house. Later she was *in*[9] her friend's house, not seeing it on a television screen or through binoculars. That space surrounded her, enveloped her, filled her with an alien presence that made her planned behavior (unpacking her sack) unreal and uncanny. As her lived space changed its character, her plans became irrelevant. Something else took over, and her friend's door began to pull as her own had done half an hour before, but with a quite different sense of urgency, as we noted in Chapter 1.

The room I am in now has a geometric space that I understand when I try to draw a map of it. I can also relate its visual presence to that conceptual space by taking account of my location. But I grasp it as a lived space most fundamentally through my behavior: The chair is where I sit, the table holds my papers and my coffee cup, the windows are to look out of—a hole is to dig. The structure of physiognomic fields blends what we know abstractly into the fabric of meaning of our experience as surely as it integrates other horizons. The immediate presence of the world to me, and of me to it, is a marvelous synthesis of meanings from temporal, spatial, interpersonal, abstract, visual, and tactile horizons, organized around a behavioral purpose that is basic to my lived experience.

CHAPTER
8

THE SELF IN TIME

Everything I do, all my behavior, has something to do with my self. As a self, I have an identity: a name, a family, a professional role, and a social security number. But I also have a past and a future; they are as much a part of my self as my name. I know who I am (now) because I know who I have been (in the past) and who I shall be (in the future). Knowing my past and future *is* knowing who I am. Because everything I do has something to do with my self, everything I do has something to do with my past and my future as well.[1]

Everything I do has something to do with my past in two senses. First, the past is related to what I do in the sense of physical causality. It is obvious, for example, that what I do is related to the fact that the food I ate yesterday caused me to have the energy today to do it. But a second, more important relation of the past to myself has to do with the fact that I *remember*. Remembering, unlike prior causes, is something I do right now; it is a conscious appropriation of the past into a self and into an identity. There is no self that does not remember a history, for remembering a personal history *is* being a self. And there is no past without a self, without a contemporaneous remembering, or misremembering, piecing together a thousand fragments into a coherent whole, constructing a context of self-consciousness within which present experience, including specific memories, makes sense.

Similarly, everything I do has something to do with the future in two senses. Physically, my body is subject to the laws of causality, so that spraining my ankle today will cause me to limp tomorrow. But more important than mechanical causes and effects are my plans, fears, hopes, wishes—anticipations in general. Unlike limping tomorrow, anticipating is something I do right now; it is the conscious appropriation of a future into a self and an identity. Being a self *is* anticipating a personal future. No self exists without it, however vague it may be. No one fails to note that he will be someplace tomorrow and next year. Even if he does not know where he will be, his life right now is based on the assumption that he has a future.[2]

My history and future, as I reckon them now, *are* who I am and how I am-in-the-world. We could say that my future and past *influence* my being in-the-world (A + B) and that my being-in-the-world *influences* my future and past (B + A). But that is an awkward way to put it, for my future and my past *are* my anticipations and memories, and my being-in-the-world *is* my anticipations and memories; hence A = B. We *are* our histories and futures as we reckon them now.[3] Being-in-the-world is a "future, making present, in the process of having been" as Martin Heidegger has put it. The concept of self as used here therefore refers to how we reckon our past and future. Such a reckoning is a matter of remembering and anticipating; some of its content is explicit, but a good deal of it is implicit. Like other horizons, it is presupposed, on the fringe of our explicit focus of attention, yet decisive for the meaning of events in our experience.

The experience of being a self in time is quite complex. Right now I have a sense of myself. What is involved in that sense of self? In Figure 9, I remember my childhood (1), and I anticipate that I shall die (2). When I

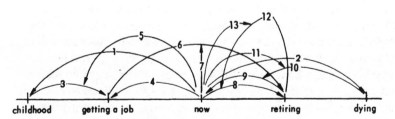

Figure 9. Schematic Representation of Being a Self in Time.

was a child, I anticipated finding a job (3), and I now remember finding the job (4); I also remember anticipating finding a job (5). My memory of how I anticipated finding a job (5) is compared to my memory of finding a job

(4), and it either lived up to my expectations, or I am somehow disappointed. I made retirement plans when I found my job (6). I now remember making them (7) and now make new ones (8). I shall look back at having done that (9), and, as I am dying, I shall remember looking back (10). I now anticipate how I shall remember remembering the retirement plans that I am making now (11).

Not all these horizons are equally important for how I understand myself in my job. But they are all implicitly part of my understanding. Occasionally one of them becomes crucial, as does my notion that when I retire I shall be amazed at how stupid my earlier retirement plans were. Part of my motivation for changing them now is that I do not want to look back and see myself as having been stupid (12). This process is anticipating remembering an anticipation (13). The diagram is complex enough to indicate how complex being a self in time really is. It is also clear that the diagram is much too simple; had I thrown in my marriage, the births of my children, the marriages of my children; my earlier physical agilities, their current decrease, and their eventual deterioration; and the hundreds of other issues that are important in my sense of myself, the diagram would rapidly have become unwieldy. Let us try to simplify all this complexity in order to be able to understand being a self in time.

BEING GUILTY

Let us consider Ms. Downs, whose being-in-the-world is burdened by guilt. Every time that she expresses anger at her children she ponders how she has hurt them. When she plays with them, she is sure that she is not giving them the love and guidance they deserve. All those playful episodes are remembered regretfully because she did not do such and such. Her judgment of herself is very harsh, for her *self is* what she remembers, and what she remembers are her failures, real and imagined. Does she remember all the bad things because her being-in-the-world is guilty? Or is her being-in-the-world guilty because she remembers only the bad things? Neither causal sequence is correct; being guilty *is* a way of remembering, and remembering the bad things is a way of being-in-the-world, that is, being guilty.[4]

But Ms. Downs also anticipates that she will continue to fail. She often avoids playing with her children because she is sure that she will disappoint them or let them down. Ms. Downs' style of living into the future does not feel to her like an unfolding of new and interesting possibilities. Rather, she expects a repetition of the past. Ms. Downs' guilt is how she *is,* and it pervades her anticipations, as well as her memories. Her self *is* what she anticipates, and what she anticipates is that she will fail once again.

Ms. Downs' guilt characterizes her being-in-the-world. Her perception of concrete fields is colored by by her expectation that they will be arenas of further failure. Her world is populated by things that remind her of what she regrets and frighten her by presenting what she fears—possibilities of failure. Guilt is, therefore, a way of being-in-the-world. It is an appropriation of the *past* in which we remember past failures, which leads us to anticipate that we shall continue to remember past failures, which leads us to remember anticipating future failures, which leads us to anticipate remembering anticipating future failures.

Ms. Downs' first remembering of past failures requires the horizon of her anticipation of future failures, and her first anticipation of future failures requires the horizon of her remembering past failures. Only on the basis of fearing does she regret, and only on the basis of regretting does she fear. Each requires the other, and each produces the other. Both are required by and require her being guilty. Regretting is a way of remembering, and fearing is a way of anticipating: together they make up being guilty, which is a way of being-in-the-world.

This process is not as complex as it sounds. Being a self is remembering a personal past and anticipating a personal future. Being guilty is a way of being a self. Schematically, it can be represented this way:

Being Guilty

remembering: regretting past failures
anticipating: fearing future failures

BEING SENTIMENTAL

Now let us consider Mr. Pinky, whose being-in-the-world is sentimental. He remembers the past through rose-colored glasses and views present events as poor imitations of an idyllic existence in former years. His wife has grown wrinkled and pudgy and, compared to the way he remembers her, quite unromantic and mundane. He cannot laugh at her jokes about her weight; there is too much at stake for him to laugh. Her presence reminds him of how glorious it all was, how handsome he looked and how beautiful she was on their wedding day. That is all gone now; a lot has changed in their twenty years together. Their neighborhood has deteriorated, prices have gone up, and even the television shows have become violent and ugly.

We might say that Mr. Pinky lives in the past, but that is not the whole story.

Mr. Pinky's sense of the future is double. On one hand, he is resigned to the facts that he and his wife will continue to grow older and less attractive and that life will repeat itself in its current dreary ordinariness. But at the same time Mr. Pinky has rich and glorious fantasies about how both could lose weight, he could be swept off his feet by his secretary, or they might find uranium in the backyard and become millionaires. These fantasies occur in the spirit of "If only it were true. . . ." He recognizes that they will not come true. These fantasies are mere wishes, constituting a fairy-tale way to make his present disappointments tolerable by living into an artificial and contrived future.

Mr. Pinky's sentimentality is how he is-in-the-world. Concrete perceptual fields are colored by his memories and his wishes. They are either beautiful repetitions of his idyllic past, stages for his fantasy future, or, most commonly, disappointing in their failure to be either. His remembering is reminiscing, his anticipating is wishing, his being-in-the-world is sentimental. When he reminisces about the self he used to be, some content comes into focus, and other content fades into oblivion. He *is* his idyllic history. But the images and content also appear against the backdrop of, and in contrast to, a sense of the present as dull and ugly.[5] As in his fantasy, his anticipations engage him in an unreal existence that runs parallel to an actual state of affairs. Being sentimental sometimes obscures this sense of the present for him. He would rather not face it. He is continually disappointed with life, but he keeps going, hiding his disappointment for the sake of his sentimentality.

Being sentimental is an appropriation of the *future* in which we anticipate future idylls, which lead us to remember anticipating future idylls, which lead us to anticipate remembering anticipating future idylls.

Mr. Pinky's remembering of past idylls requires the horizon of his wishing for future idylls, and his wishing for future idylls requires the horizon of remembering past idylls. Only on the basis of wishing do we reminisce, and only on the basis of reminiscing do we wish. Each requires the other, and each produces the other. Both are required by and require being sentimental. Reminiscing is a way of remembering, and wishing is a way of anticipating, and together they make up being sentimental, which is a way of being-in-the-world. Schematically, it can be represented this way:

Being Sentimental

remembering: reminiscing about past idylls
anticipating: wishing for future idylls

IDENTITY AND FREEDOM

In contrast to objects that do not experience, how I am currently being in the world shapes my history. When I am regretting things past, certain aspects of my history loom up to define me; from the entire array of remembered fragments, certain ones form the *Gestalt* of self, whereas others fade into oblivion. When I am reminiscing, in contrast, certain other aspects of my history become salient and support my being that way by giving me a different self to be. In the course of a single day, I may be many selves, each producing and being produced by a pattern of memories. But over the course of days and years I gather together some aspects of my history that are always present, whether I am regretting or reminiscing. These stable elements appear as biographical facts and my relation to them is one of neutral recall. They form whatever stable self is always there through the vicissitudes of regret and reminiscence. They are a ballast of continuing identity, and I cling to them as I cling to my identity. I was born in such and such a town of certain parents, went to certain schools, and have done this and that over the course of several decades. I remember these items, always have and always will. Their pattern changes somewhat over the years; which high school I went to is not as important now as it once was, but the stability of these facts is important in my ability to know who I am. These biographical facts are a mere skeleton of my self, however. The *way* I remember them may be full of regret or reminiscence. Their meanings may vary, depending on whether I am regretting or reminiscing.

In the instances of Ms. Downs and Mr. Pinky, their *ways* of remembering their pasts have evolved into a kind of chronic regretting and chronic reminiscing respectively. They could change their ways of remembering, and therefore they could change the meanings of these biographical facts for them if, and only if, their current being-in-the-world were to change. Indeed, for Ms. Downs to remember her past differently would be for her to be less guilty. For Mr. Pinky to remember his past differently would be for him to be less sentimental.

The circumstances under which I say or feel that I know who I am are pointed into a future. When I am uncertain about my future, about what to do next or in the long run, it is because I am uncertain about who I am and have been. Both Ms. Downs and Mr. Pinky are *too certain* about who they have been. They know what their pasts and futures are. They lack our more usual uncertainty. Such uncertainty is essential to freedom and expresses a kind of fluidity and flexibility in one's relation to one's past. It is the absence of this uncertainty that fixes Ms. Downs' and Mr. Pinky's histories—and their futures. This kind of fixedness may appear either as a pathological compulsion to repeat or a fear of repeating what is regretted, as in the instance of Ms. Downs. Or it may appear as an unquestioned confidence of repeating, or wishing to repeat, what is reminisced, as in the instance of Mr. Pinky. In fearing and wishing, Ms. Downs and Mr. Pinky are binding the future by binding the past; they cling to the past and thus reduce uncertainty, but they therefore find themselves being guilty and sentimental respectively, with no freedom to become what they have not been or to have been what they do not expect to become.

Naturally, Ms. Downs and Mr. Pinky are extremes. They have limited their own freedom in clear and unnecessary ways. Being guilty or being sentimental does not have to pervade our being-in-the-world the way it does for them. But we all have some of Ms. Downs and Mr. Pinky in us; we all are guilty and sentimental to some extent. In trying to describe being-in-the-world or self in time, we have established some terminology for talking about it. We have characterized two ways of being-in-the-world and described typical ways of remembering and anticipating for each, of being our past and our future:

Being Guilty

remembering: regretting
anticipating: fearing

Being Sentimental

remembering: reminiscing
anticipating: wishing

Obviously, this list does not exhaust how we remember or anticipate or how we are. But, as we all are guilty and sentimental to some extent, the description helps us to see how these postures matter for who we are in time.

Let us describe a third way of being-in-the-world, which is also universal, though typical of each of us to varying degrees. We want to describe what is involved in being free, being practical, being "healthy" (as we often put it in our culture). We shall call this kind of remembering *recall* and this kind of anticipating *hope*. Just as wishing and reminiscing imply each other and as fearing and regretting imply each other, so do hoping and recalling imply each other. Being into the future (hoping) and being into the past (recalling) are horizons for each other; they require each other and are required by each other. The past we live and the future we live are part of each other in the structure of human experience. They are both aspects of our being-in-the world, which is being a self in time.

First, hoping is living into the future in an open-ended way. In hoping, the future is not limited or constricted by the past; my anticipations are not repetitions; an envisioned future is a creative product, not a reproduction of aspects of my past. Neither Ms. Downs nor Mr. Pinky can create in this way.

Second, hoping points us into a future that is continuous with the present in a practical way. Decisions I make now are meaningful because of their practical relation to a future that is understood to be possible but not inevitable. Hope contrasts with Ms. Downs' fears in that she did not feel that her decisions mattered. Everything would always be the same. Hope contrasts with Mr. Pinky's wishing in that it is practical and behavioral and that it motivates action in the public world. Neither Ms. Downs nor Mr. Pinky can make decisions with the thought that they will follow them through behaviorally and that this behavior will make a difference to who and how they are.

Third, hoping creates a future against the horizon of an *expanding* past, a past whose richness and complexity continually renew the meanings and options of the future, whereas fearing and wishing produce a future against the horizon of a past that is becoming progressively narrower and well-defined, progressively *constricted* in its content. Sometimes, therefore, we live into a future hopefully, which means, first, that we envision something new in the future; second, that it will come about because of practical steps we can take now; and, third, that it will supply a new point of view from which to reckon the meaning of our own past.

 Hoping also implies a certain way of living into the past, that is, recalling. First, recalling is an appropriation of an open-ended past. In recalling, the past is not constricted to thematic content like idylls and failures, and the biographical events recalled do not have the permanent meaning of idylls or failures but can change meaning with new interpretations and perspectives. In recalling, therefore, I am continually creating a new past that is not limited by fearful or wishful anticipations. Ms. Downs' past, in contrast, always means failure to her, and so she cannot anticipate a future hopefully but is filled with fear. Mr. Pinky's past is always idyllic, and so his future can mean only fantasized repetition or disappointment.

Second, recalling brings forth a past that is continuous with the present in a practical way. Neither regretting nor reminiscing has this practical continuity. Decisions made now by Ms. Downs and Mr. Pinky may be meaningful in relation to their regretted or reminisced pasts, but the continuity is not a practical one; it is a fantasied one. It is fantastic for Ms. Downs to do penance for a regretted past out of fear of repetition, and it is fantastic for Mr. Pinky ritualistically to bind himself to a reminisced past out of wishing for a repetition of it. In contrast, decisions made now in relation to a *recalled* past become meaningful in that they will change the sum total of my past in the future and make the best of what cannot be changed, thus in effect changing it; they will build upon, rather than try to undo or repeat the past.

Third, recalling creates a past against the horizon of an *expanding* future, a future whose open-endedness promises continual re-creation of the meaning of the past, whereas regretting and reminiscing produce a past against the horizon of a future that, in being feared or wished, becomes progressively narrower and constricted in its thematic content. Sometimes, therefore, we live into the past in recall, which means, first, that the meaning of the past is subject to change, even though the events themselves are over; second, that our decisions now build upon but do not try to undo or repeat the past; and, third, that such a past supplies a point of view from which the future can continue to expand.

Being free or healthy (or whatever we want to call it) is characterized by creatively reforming meanings as we continually change, thus leaving us in a constant state of flux as to who we have been, are, and are becoming.[6] It also builds upon this constantly changing past in a practical way, avoiding the fantasies of penance born of fearing or regretting and of repetition born of wishing or reminiscing. The horizonal character of both past and future, each a horizon for the other, makes for a continual opening of possibilities in both past and future. As my anticipations become more hopeful, more options appear in my future, which supplies a horizon against which more interpretations of the past become possible. And, as my remembering becomes more one of recall, more interpretations of the past appear, which supplies a horizon against which more future options become possible.

It is unreasonable to label all experiences of regret and reminiscence "pathological," for they are quite inevitable in human experience. But we must also note that regret and reminiscence engage us not only with a past but also with a present and a future as well, indeed with a self in time, a being-in-the-world. Any single person will be-in-the-world in a variety of ways over a period of time. What we call "psychopathological" is a matter of one's identity, or self in time. There is a tendency for those so labeled to have a center of gravity of their identity in regret, or reminiscence, or both, to become locked into a self-definition that allows no redefinition and hence no sense of freedom. If the psychotherapeutic task with respect to the future is to transform wishing and fearing into hoping, it is also to transform regretting and reminiscing into recalling. And, as past and future are always mutually horizonal, these two transformations must and do occur together. What is most essentially transformed is neither one's past nor one's future alone, but one's being-in-the-world that past and future make up.

The sense of freedom that we can have is always limited. I can build upon my past in a variety of ways, each creating a somewhat different past in the future. But I am not free to invent my past extravagantly[7] without becoming deluded about who I am. My daughter, who was hopeful (according to our lengthy definition) during the first part of the evening, became wishful; she changed her identity from "growing up" to the more sentimental "little girl." Unlike Mr. Pinky, she can have her way. Children are perhaps freer to do that kind of thing when they overextend themselves than adults are, because we expect less consistency from children and because the child's experience of self is less stabilized. Deciding how free we should be in this respect requires a value judgment, but we can surely recommend my daughter's flexibility over Ms. Downs' and Mr. Pinky's inflexibility. They are unhappy people who cannot change their sense of themselves sufficiently to justify such behavioral inconsistencies as my daughter produced. On the other hand, adults who behave as my daughter did are likely to be seen as childish, inconsistent, inconsiderate of others, and difficult to live with. If Ms. Downs and Mr. Pinky are extremes of too well-defined selves, then an adult who behaves as may daughter did approaches the opposite extreme of too loosely defined a self to sustain interpersonal agreements, to which we now turn.

CHAPTER

9

INTERPERSONAL AGREEMENTS

Recalling again my daughter's episode described in Chapter 1, we find that her behavior, when she changed her mind, was not histrionic; it was not a dramatic production for the sake of a dramatic production. To be sure, her crying was produced in part because she wanted to come home, and she had some understanding that crying and saying that she wanted to come home would result in her being *allowed* to come home. Her behavior was intended to produce the results it produced, and in this sense it was a display intended for the eyes of others. But the critical message "I want to go home" was straightforward and true. I can confidently report, on the other hand, that she is not always so straightforward. There are definitely times when she cries when she is with her brothers, not because she is hurt, frightened, or anxious that her stated desires be fulfilled, but because she knows her crying will gain her some attention from her parents or perhaps can be used as a threat against her brothers to draw her parents to her side and to have her way. Put another way, the physiognomy of her friend's room was such that she could not stay there, so she cried to come home. At other times, her field is structured with a definite audience, and crying becomes a manipulative technique, responsive to a political space in which it is designed merely to gain allies—a field and a movement in that field very different from those on the night she changed her mind.

Standing outside her experience, observing her behavior, it is sometimes easy and sometimes difficult to make a judgment about the interpersonal structure of her field. A sure tip-off is seeing her cry only as long as her mother can hear her and as soon as her mother is out of range, seeing her cease to cry and resume her play—a good deal less upset than her crying would have led me to believe. At other times, I may treat her crying as if it were merely a manipulative technique in a space of allies and loyalties when it is really an expression of hurt or fright. I interpret her space wrongly and see it as histrionic when it is straightforward. At other times I make the opposite mistake, because I think she is hurt or frightened: I am taken in by a histrionic display and allow myself to be manipulated in a power game in which she wants me to join forces with her against her brothers. Even though we more or less frequently make such errors, our responses to our children's crying is always determined by such judgments. Their crying means to us X or Y, depending on how we interpret the physiognomies of their spaces, which in turn is based on how we understand their being-in-the-world.

There are also, of course, intermediate instances. Certainly it is true of older people that both straightforward and histrionic meanings may be present simultaneously. For example, I may behave *as if* I am frightened in order to achieve some other aim (like winning sympathy) and then come to structure my perceptual field in a frightening way. Or, if I characteristically get my way by being angry, I may come to see my field as offensive, provoking anger, and justifying anger. Here my physiognomic field has been accommodated to a political one. My anger has *both* meanings simultaneously: one meaning in a space between myself and whatever made me angry, another meaning in a space between myself and another person who is intimidated by or sympathetic to my anger. Such complications are more the rule and less the exception, especially in adult experience. We can see how the physiognomic field integrates and synthesizes those horizons that we separate for analysis. And we can also see how it participates in a larger "style," or *modus operandi,* that we understand as being-in-the-world.[1]

It is the purpose of this chapter to establish some terminology with which we can understand behavior in terms of its interpersonal horizons. We shall speak of "agreements" as a way to describe those implicit and unspoken understandings shared by people who have to face one another. Often such agreements come into focus most vividly in their violation. We all know people who seem to be "on another wavelength," whose judgments about proper and agreeable behavior are different from ours.

Such agreements may occur very locally, as in a two-person group that has existed for a while, and they may have nothing to do with a larger group ("John might have said X, but I'm sure he would not violate *our* relationship by violating our trust"). Or they may occur on a somewhat larger scale, as in a family ("A Rockefeller would not do that"), a clique, or social group ("Everyone knows what you can expect from a Sigma Chi"). Still others are ethnic and even national.[2] Naturally, the smaller groups and their agreements are more amenable to close analysis.

DYADS

Let us suppose that my reaction to my daughter, on the night she changed her mind, had been to say: "Oh come on now, you don't want to come home. You want to stay." What would the essential message have been? I would have been telling her that I did not believe her protestations. I would have been saying that I knew her mind better than she did. I would have been disqualifying her expressed desires and claiming that what she thought she felt was not what she *really* felt. I would have been telling her that, whatever being-in-the-world she was enacting, her desire to come home was not real. Such a move, if pressed and maintained by me, would have undercut my daughter's own ability to believe in her own experience.

We all do that to our children from time to time, but we also let them "have their way," follow their immediate sense of things, and thus give them the message "The little girl whom you are enacting is really you" or "Your immediate experience is believable and trustworthy and should be respected as presented." Such a response, which is about what I expressed after some initial hesitation and feelings of annoyance, is a *confirmation*. It establishes the agreement, not only to let the child be who she is being, but also to confirm that identity, to confirm the experience from which it is derived, to accept and approve of who she was being in that situation.

We sometimes confirm others, and sometimes we do not, depending on whether or not we see their behavior as straightforward, which in turn depends on whether we think the being-in-the-world expressed in that behavior is real and, if real, is tolerable to us. To have denied my daughter confirmation of her being a "little girl" might have enabled her to regain her former identity as "growing up," and perhaps that would have been the better fatherly response. We shall never know. But we all know what it feels like to be confirmed and to be disconfirmed. If you see yourself as a bright student, a professor can confirm or disconfirm your judgment of yourself and the legitimacy of the experience upon which it is based. We have all had the experience that one of our *pretensions* has been disconfirmed because the other whom we wanted to convince somehow let us know that he was not convinced.

Often we offer confirmation to another with the implicit expectation that we shall enjoy a return on our offering. I permitted my daughter to be a little girl, and this lenience obligated her to confirm my sense of myself as her father. If you persuade a professor to agree that you are not very smart, he may grant you that pretension in return for your confirming his view of himself as dazzlingly intelligent. A wife may pretend that she is weak, for this pretense allows her to avoid certain kinds of responsibilities, and she may be able to persuade her husband to agree to that definition of her if she agrees to confirm his pretense that he is very strong. A boy may enact the role of "one who is deeply troubled" and evoke confirmation from his girl friend in exchange for confirming her view of herself as one who ministers to the deeply troubled.

Such agreements are often very local, unique to a particular relationship; they may reflect very personal fantasies or culturally defined roles. To the extent that they involve pretensions, each party becomes locked into a view of the other that is static and depends on ignoring contrary evidence. Such agreements are called *collusions;* they "feel" like a mutual understanding that one can trust, but they also "feel" confining. For the "very strong" husband to decide that he is not so strong and to demand more strength from his wife is to try to change and, in changing, to violate the agreement. Many relationships break up because one or the other member decides for some reason to change and to change his view of the other. We are most vividly aware of such agreements when they are broken.

Collusion is when two people agree to confirm each other's pretensions.[3] The experience of having my pretense confirmed is also an experience of being obligated; I can feel the obligation to return the favor when someone confirms my pretense. If I conform to the implicit agreement, a definite spatial structure is established between me and thee. Rules, implicit and unspoken—even unspeakable—can be felt. Certain reactions become legitimate, and others do not. I become obliged, for example, to continue to ignore evidence that contradicts the other's pretense and to refrain from behavior that too seriously contradicts my own pretense. One of the crucial skills we all learn in growing up is how to establish and maintain such agreements. We must be sensitive to what the other wants us to think; we must be careful not to say too much, for speaking the unspoken is a violation, and we must know how to let the other know which of our pretenses are important to us.

If having an image of myself confirmed when it really should not be gives me the experience of obligation, then being disconfirmed by another gives me the experience of *shame.* Certainly one of the weapons available to us when we want to hurt someone is to evoke shame. But the experience of presenting my pretense for confirmation and not receiving it does not have to be a sudden feeling that something is ruptured. When we first meet someone who withholds confirmation, we are likely to feel only a vague sense of failure of our inability to establish rapport, to "get through" to him. Sometimes we respect that withholding from others (as when we have some sense that our pretense is really a pretense), and sometimes we avoid future encounters. Sometimes both.

If confirmation is withheld when we are not pretending or have no sense that we are, we may feel *pain*. It is a strange kind of social pain, not because something is wrong with our bodies but because something is wrong with our relationships. The structure that supplies the horizon for this pain is not our sense of physical well-being but our sense of social well-being. Social pain can be every bit as painful as physical pain.

The experience of not pretending and being confirmed is the experience of being understood. We like people with whom we doff our pretensions and who accept us nevertheless. We trust them because we sense that they trust us. They look genuine to us, and we feel genuine to them. We know that they know how they look to us and how we feel we look to them. Being confirmed in our nonpretensious selves is always a relative or approximate matter, for a total unmasking of pretensions is rare indeed. But the experience of trusting and being trusted in the context of mutual nonpretentious confirmation is the mainstay of human morale and rapport. All of us have experienced some of it; all of us want more.

LARGER GROUPS

The social space in which we move is structured according to groups larger than dyadic relationships. The prototypical small group, and perhaps the most powerful, is the primary family.[4] Families are hardly all alike, yet it is possible to locate some horizons that are nearly universal because they are part of the experience of being a family member. Being a family member often involves an obligation not unlike that in collusion. A family is not a random collection of individuals; it is a group that has some very definite agreements. The most important agreement is that we all identify ourselves as members. In operational terms, this requirement means that we all agree to expect agreements from one another. A family is a group of people who agree that there are agreements. It is this agreement *that* there are agreements, more than the specific agreements themselves, that holds the family together. The greatest threat to a family's cohesion comes, not from disagreements or from different versions of what the agreements are, but from challenges to the existence of the agreements themselves.[5] Indeed, to say that there are no agreements is to say that there is no family but only a collection of individuals. "I disagree with everything you say, but you are still my father" is a less threatening statement than, "I agree with some of what you say (or all of it), but that is no big deal; I also agree with Mr. Smith." The former expresses an agreement about who these people *are* to each other; the latter denies it. To say the latter, and to mean it, is to announce that there is no family for me; it is to violate the agreement that makes the family a family.

Most families (and other cohesive small groups) also have agreements with certain content that is more or less important and certain rituals for the continuing confirmation of the existence of the family. For some families, eating together is sacred as an expression of continued mutual commitment; for others, merely keeping one another informed in a casual (but sufficiently "thoughtful") way is sufficient. The content of agreements sometimes amounts to elaborate myths, and sometimes the rituals (like eating) are concrete enactments of these myths (like the notion that the parents are the source of all things good and wholesome).

Small, cohesive groups can be quite tyrannical. Refusal to perform the rituals, open disagreement about the myth, or especially denial that there are agreements is subject to serious reprisal. The more the family members depend on the existence and continuity of the family in order to sustain their own identities, the more vindictively they will respond to deviant members. Although it may seem easier to be cruel to strangers, some of the most vicious cruelty emerges within small groups of people who know one another very well, for in trying to keep their groups together they are protecting their own sense of who they are.[6]

Family myths and rituals may well focus on some implicit division of labor in the family. Roles evolve as localized versions of culturally defined roles,[7] and people interpret one another's behavior against the backdrop of role expectations. But labor is not the only thing that is divided and organized. Power, love, ecstasy, tolerance, and other interpersonal commodities are distributed according to a particular pattern for a particular family, and this pattern is agreed upon by family members. "John is the studious one, Jim the delinquent; Sally is your daughter, and Jane is mine." Of course, this distribution is unspoken, but should Jim try to play John's role, he would be violating the agreement and perhaps threatening family members' sense of who they are.

Understanding family myths and rituals, as well as the nature of the agreements that exist in a particular family, is most obviously critical for understanding behavior that occurs in the presence of family itself. When *they* are present, the agreements constitute a powerful horizon in individual experience, and, in order to understand what behavior in the family means to the various members, we must understand the agreements. But, even outside the family setting, we carry our family's myths and rituals with us. The family we grew up in therefore remains important in terms of the kinds of agreements we enter into and what these agreements mean to us. Similarly, a small group like a social clique in high school or college—with its agreements, myths, and rituals—is most important when we try to understand behavior that occurs in the presence of that group. But, like the family, it contributes something to our ability to form and sustain those implicit agreements that hold social life together.

In understanding behavior phenomenologically, therefore, we can focus our attention on interpersonal agreements as one kind of horizon that always matters. But this horizon is hardly separable from the contemporaneous physical space and its physiognomy, as discussed in Chapter 7, or from being a self in longitudinal time, as discussed in Chapter 8. A contemporaneous physical space is a physiognomy highly colored by interpersonal agreements, as when we feel the pull toward a lover or the push from someone who will not confirm us. Being a self in time is colored by the same kinds of agreements; Ms. Downs almost certainly has achieved implicit agreements with others in order to confirm her culpability, perhaps trading on her willingness to see others as innocent and good. The relations among all these kinds of horizons are intricate and complex. Perhaps it would be even more accurate to say that there are no such *relations* because these horizons are usually not separated in our lived experience.

Lived experience is as it is, and we must always return to it in order to understand behavior. Our experience synthesizes with consummate creativity[8] these kinds of horizons discussed here separately. The relation between the level of interpersonal agreements and that of physiognomic space, for example, is not very well captured by such terms as *influenced* and *colored*. One does not cause the other, nor does it "sort of cause" the other, as these terms suggest. One is horizonal for the other; it supplies the backdrop against which the other level can have its meaning to us. I may say, therefore, that an impulsive act by Ms. Downs (for example, a suicide attempt) has meaning against the backdrop of her physiognomic field (perhaps she perceives an obstacle to overcome). That field is as it is in her experience only against the backdrop of her interpersonal agreements (perhaps a promise that both she and the other person do not expect her to succeed in keeping), but these agreements are as they are in her experience only against the backdrop of her being in time ("I have been and always will be a failure"). Furthermore, this particular stacking of horizons, which most vividly reflects the meanings of her act, may be different at another time, in another place, with another act. A phenomenological analysis cannot be limited only to a list of *levels of meaning;* it must reveal a picture of the structure of the experience of an event in its uniqueness. The most general term we have, which is always the most basic horizon of meaning in human experience, is *being-in-the-world.* The unique structure of one's being-in-the-world differs from person to person and also (but less so) from moment to moment. The levels of space, time, and other people are always part of being-in-the-world, but they never play exactly the same role. In Chapters 7–9 we have described universal horizons, but their place in a phenomenological analysis must be determined by the structure of each in experience (or the structure of experience in the event, we may say), not by preconceived theory.[9]

PART
IV

CONCLUSION

CHAPTER
10

THE WORLD

Inevitably, when we ask about the "relations" among the universal horizons described in Part III, we are confronted with a conceptual puzzle that cannot be solved on a conceptual level. The three horizons—space, time, and others—may be universal because behavior and experience are always oriented within a physical, personal, and social context. But they are separable horizons or contexts for analytic purposes only. They do not have to be related conceptually, because they occur simultaneously in experience, and we want our concepts to be true to experience.

Each of these horizons is an aspect of the *world*, but the world is not a sum of these parts. It is the more fundamental horizon within which these horizons can be made visible in phenomenological analysis, against which they appear, from which they have been abstracted, and by virtue of which there is experience *at all*. The world is therefore not an easy concept; it is so fundamental to experience that it is very difficult to call it into question and thus to see its importance. Already in Chapter 2 we offered some hints on the nature of the world. We want now to go into more detail about this horizon of horizons.

THE WORLD AS EXPERIENCE

If you are walking about a city where you have been for only a few days, you keep your bearings in order not to become lost. The park is always on

103

your left or behind you when you turn right. The skyscraper across from the park will be visible at any rate. And from it you can find Market Street, where the critical bus line runs. If by chance you wander into a part of the city where the skyscraper is not visible and you become confused about whether you turned right once or twice (or was it right once and then left?), then something changes. Buildings that were being mapped by you before, located in a space that was oriented, now loom up in a kind of locationless presence. Still, that red building is between the blue and silver one, even if you do not know where they are with respect to the skyscraper anymore. If you panic at being lost, even the order of the blue, red, and silver buildings loses its orienting power, and you feel the eerie sense of endless streets, all of which lead somewhere meaningless to you. It is an unpleasant feeling, one you try to resolve. You try to find yourself, for being lost is upsetting. You want to know how to find that critical bus line.

Such an experience demonstrates clearly enough the variations in the appearance and meanings of buildings and streets, according to variations in the spatial "frame" we put them in. But even in our mild discomfort at being temporarily lost, there is still a framework that allows buildings and streets to have meaning. You know you are *temporarily* lost, for you have not walked that far, and you can always ask someone the way. The experience is thus embedded in a framework of time that remains reliable and promises that you will find yourself again. And you note that, after walking around the blue, red, and silver buildings, they appear silver-red-blue in a left-to-right sequence because you are on the other side. Space, too, though no longer anchored by your knowledge of where the bus line runs, remains consistent. Furthermore, people rush about, going to and from places in a fashion that is familiar. So what if you are lost? There is nothing uncanny about that.

Suppose, however, that you discover that no matter what point you view the buildings from, they are always blue, red, and silver from left to right. They must be moving! Or your movement in space is no longer having its usual effect upon your visual experience. Suppose that the faster you run toward the policeman, the farther away he becomes, even though he is standing still. Suppose that it is growing earlier rather than later, that it is in fact a different day, snowing whereas it had been summer before. Suppose that the people, instead of going places in a familiar way, are all looking at you, whispering to one another, occasionally sharing suppressed laughter.

Being lost is one thing; most of the world hangs together nevertheless. Spatial, temporal, and social coordinates of meaning are still intact, and the world continues to make sense. But these other experiences are something else. Spatial, temporal, and social coordinates are no longer reliable. The world, as we usually depend upon it in order to situate ourselves, dissolves. When these coordinates dissolve, the world dissolves; when the world dissolves, our ability to situate ourself dissolves and with it the given network of meanings upon which we so blithely (but in fact desperately) rely.

But even these experiences are frightening, different, and uncanny because we compare them to a remembered standard of coherence. Even in the midst of this panic, the world is implicitly still there—in its absence. There is no experience at all without the world, and incidently there is no *world* (in the phenomenological sense) at all without experience.

Edmund Husserl (1970) called the "world" *Lebenswelt*, the "life-world," or lived-world. This world is not an alien place into which we are thrown at random, hostile to our survival and indifferent to our experience. It is the world of everyday existence: familiar things, rooms, streets, people, and activities. It is the world as appropriated by human beings, interpreted and shaped in its very presence according to who we are—even as who we are is interpreted and shaped according to the world's already given presence.

It is the world that we live *in,* but the world is more than a place; it is an *experience.* As experience, the world is neither inside our heads (merely "subjective") nor outside ourselves (merely "objective"). Experience binds an organism to its environment; it is the channel of communication between them, the means by which each is present for the other. The world is present for me because I experience, and experience is there because the world is there. The world is thus not just *an* experience; the world is experience itself.

The world, like experience, is not "out there" (merely "objective"), neutral and meaningless. On the contrary in my everyday life I find the world full of meanings, meanings that are always already there, not created by me and not merely subjective but also not separate from me and not merely objective.[1] I am *in* the world, but by virtue of experience the world is also *in* me; the world and I interpenetrate each other. I am who I am only because of the world, and the world is who and what it is only because of me and you and the rest of the conscious beings who appropriate it.

THE WORLD AS AN ONTOLOGICAL PROBLEM

When we think of my daughter's episode reported in Chapter 1, we do not know which objects stood out from the field and became salient parts of her change of mind. Perhaps all the objects looked different, and the character of the field itself changed. Simultaneously (as both cause and effect though these terms are not very appropriate), her sense of herself changed from that of an incipient planning adult to a little girl. Her world changed from a set of meanings that supported her growing up to a set of meanings that supported her understanding herself as a little girl. The meanings of the immediate field, of time and space, of objects and people, of herself and the world all changed at once. All are aspects of the *world*, that context of meanings within which the field, objects, people, self, and so on have their meanings. When we say that she changed her mind, we mean to say that her world changed.

At this point, we may focus our attention on what changed, or we may be interested in what stayed the same. She still identified herself as my daughter, the houses as theirs and ours, the time as bedtime, and so on. She changed from understanding herself as a growing version of a planning adult to a little girl nestling in protective covers in her own house, but she re- mained embedded in the same world, with the same identity. She was not amnesic nor insanely convinced that she was someone else. The sameness throughout the episode, the stability of the complex of world, identity, field, and object is as remarkable as the change. We are less likely to notice this consistency, for we have come to expect and assume it—about my daughter, any other person, and ourselves. Yet, if we want to explore and understand human experience, this sameness is just as impressive a datum as is the change.

Descriptive phenomenological work always ferrets out horizons that allow a phenomenon to stand out and be experienced. Seeking the horizons of horizons ultimately leads us back to the world, which is always there, full of meaning, supplying the context or frame within which meaningful experiences emerge. When we are impressed with the sameness, the continu- ity, and universality of experience like the stability of identity and the world throughout my daughter's episode—we are bound to ask the question "How is it possible that there are the world, meaning, and experience at all?" It is a profound question about the being of anything at all or about being in general. When philosophers take up this question, they are explor- ing *ontology*, the study of being.[2]

Our explorations of my daughter's episode, on the other hand, were less ontological and more *ontic*. We were more concerned with this particular person than with human beings in general, and, furthermore, we were more concerned with a particular episode of change than with her characteristic being-in-the-world in general. We did, however, have to refer to her general understanding of herself in order to make the specific episode lucid, and we did have to refer to the ontological facts of the world in order to make lucid her general understanding of herself. The ontological questions of being in general is never far from the surface as soon as we begin exploring the intricacies of a particular human situation.[3]

THE COMMONALITY OF THE WORLD

Suppose that you see two tired and sweating tennis players leave the tennis court and enter a bar across the street. This observed behavior has a fairly clear reference and a number of contexts that are immediately clear to us. We understand the behavior because its meaning, from the participants' point of view, is fairly unambiguous. We understand the social ritual of drinking together after playing tennis together, the visual field of the street and the inviting quality of the bar, the physical sensation of being hot and thirsty, and so on. All these aspects are immediately understandable, and, although we may be wrong (perhaps they are really going in to rob the proprietor), we depend upon such understandings, some more and some less elaborate, in our everyday lives. Such understandings depend on the shared meanings of social rituals, bars, and thirst. We have these meanings in common with the tennis players.

Suppose that you are one of the tennis players. You see your friend's fatigue and discomfort as you feel your own, and you offer to buy him a cold beer. You expect that he will accept, politely decline, or insist on buying you one too; you do not expect him to fly into a rage, ignore your offer, or take off his clothes and stand on his head. The expectations of him that you have are known to him, and you know that he knows you have them. They are a part of a shared set of rules of propriety that enable us to get along with one another every day.

Suppose that you were me, the father of my daughter, and that you received the telephone call that your daughter had been crying for half an hour after her eagerly anticipated arrival at her friend's house. In this instance, your expectations would have been violated, as mine were, and you would recognize that there was something you did not understand. Why did she change her mind?

Even asking that question is, however, based upon a previously shared understanding of your daughter's anticipation. To call it a "change of mind" is to understand, first, that she wanted to go and, second, that she wanted to come home. Both wanting to go and wanting to come home are understandable; you may not know *why* she changed her mind, but you know what wanting to go and wanting to come home are like. You share with her a number of meanings of the space (home and away from home) and the time (remembering, wanting now, anticipating, and so on). Furthermore, the commonality of understanding you have with your daughter is vividly demonstrated by the fact that you *ask* why she changed her mind as soon as the understanding is ruptured. You are thrown into puzzlement as soon as the commonality disappears.

Throughout our everyday experience, at its very basis, is a commonly held set of meanings, collectively organized into the world, implicitly shared with others, and absolutely decisive for our being who and how we are. The world—spatial, temporal, interpersonal, shared, always there—is at the basis of all our understanding of ourselves and one another. Most of the fundamental characteristics of the world are given to us; we become "hooked" on them as a frame of meaning for our entire lives long before we can critically reflect on what or how they are. The world is always already there.[4]

That which is always already there in our experience consists of more than mere objects like physical entities or patches of light and dark, hard and soft, sweet and sour. Always already there is a prior set of meanings, a totality of reference within which everything else makes sense. I may understand the tennis players, my daughter, or you—but only as part of an already-existing prior understanding of the world. And I know that the prior understanding that I have is, in essential ways, the same as the prior understanding that you, my daughter, and the sweating tennis players have. The world is common to us, even as our perspectives on it differ and make us different people.[5]

We often assume that our minds are private compartments, known to others only to the extent that we choose to share their contents with others.[6] We recognize that we share a common world with others, but we seem also to assume that this commonality is the *result* of our sharing our private mental contents with one another. Quite the opposite assumption is possible: The commonality of the world is not the result of our sharing our experiences; it is the *basis* of doing so. My world is like yours not because we have shared our privacy; it was already like yours, and it is only because of this prior similarity that a sharing of private perspectives on it is possible.

We may ask how we can be sure of this view and also whether or not it matters.

The data leading to this conclusion come from a phenomenological analysis. The contents of my experience have a commonality with yours because *the world* (nearly synonymous with *experience*) is given to me *as our common world* (it appears that way in my experience). The world is given that way to you too. We both assume therefore that we are referring to the same world, and this common assumption *permits* us to talk. It is the basis of our talking, not the result of our talking.

The importance of this conclusion is no less than that of the ontological posture that we assume in talking about communication at all. The tension between our everyday experience and our theoretical constructions about it, as pointed out especially in Chapter 3, arises from an ontological posture that has not undergone phenomenological critcism. The issue (of "other minds") is far too complex to enter into here, but it is far from a purely academic issue, and the phenomenological notion of a common world, always already given, bears directly upon it.

VARIATIONS IN THE WORLD

Our analysis of my daughter's episode is an example of doing psychology phenomenologically. We have obviously been engaged in a double task, describing her particular world and describing the universals of the world according to which we can understand her particular being-in-the-world in that episode. To focus our attention on the role of the world in particular experiences is the best way to become sensitive to the pervading influence of the world in all human beings. Consider, for example, the experience of moods.

My world is different from day to day; we often express such a fact by saying that we experience different moods. When I examine the experience of different moods, I find that what I mean by the term "mood" is a variation in the appearance of the world.[7] I recently heard of an experience from a student, who had fallen in love with a girl during a week-long conference in a city neither had visited before. For him the city took on a magical quality—different from every other city that he had been in. The trees were greener, the sky bluer, the buildings more splendid, and so on. At one point in the week, he asked the girl what was to become of their relationship. She responded with a conventional and noncommittal sentiment that the future did not count and that she was just enjoying the present. That was not how *he* felt, and upon hearing her answer he was disappointed, yet he pretended to agree and to go along with her conventional view. For the next hour and a half, before he finally blew up in a fit of rage and nearly tore a railing from a wall, he experienced the world very differently. The trees and sky became drab, the buildings ugly; people seemed to him reckless and unpredictable, whereas they had formerly appeared friendly and comfortable. The magic of the city was gone, to be sure, but it was not just a return to a neutral city. The order and sense that had permeated the city, the people, and events were gone. The city became an alien, unwelcoming, and hostile place.

Everyone has experienced such physiognomic flip-flops. During extreme periods, it is easy to see that events are magical or hostile against the backdrop of an entire landscape that is magical or hostile. The world changes, and events take on different meanings. What are we to make of this difference? Even more to the point, however, are the meanings of events when we are *not* experiencing extremes in mood. The world has a characteristic appearance and is a network of meanings for everyday life as well. Its physiognomy may not come to our attention because it is so ordinary; a fish is the last one to discover water. Yet this physiognomy is no less powerful in framing and giving meaning to events than when we are experiencing an extreme mood.

In our ontic phenomenological psychology, in other words, we seek to arrive at an understanding of different individuals, as well as of different moods within the same individual. A description of the individual's world is just as appropriate to the former task as it is to the latter. Ludwig Binswanger (1958a) describes a number of patients in terms of their world. Let us recapitulate some of Binswanger's description to illustrate. One twenty-one-year-old woman was subject to anxiety attacks each time someone mentioned heels or shoes—a puzzling symptom indeed. But she had experienced her first anxiety and fainting spell at age five years, when her heel had become stuck in her skate and separated from her shoe. Analysis of her fantasies suggested that separation from her mother, perhaps even the birth trauma, was an important part of her history. But to say that the birth trauma, or even the skating accident, had *caused* her symptom is awkward and false. The fantasies before and after the skating accident already carried the theme of anxiety over separation. Binswanger proposes to "investigate the world-design which made possible those fantasies and phobias in the first place."

> What serves as a clue to the world-design of our little patient is the category of *continuity*, of continuous connection and containment. This entails a tremendous constriction, simplification, and depletion of the "world content," of the extremely complex totality of the patient's contexts of reference. Everything that makes the world significant is submitted to the rule of that *one* category which alone supports her "world" and being. This is what causes the great anxiety about any disruption of continuity, any gap, tearing or separating,

being separated or torn. This is why separation from the mother, experienced by everyone as the arch-separation in human life, had to become so prevalent that any event of separation served to symbolize the fear of separation from the mother and to invite and activate those phantasies and daydreams. (1958a, p. 203)

Binswanger adds that this theory is no "explanation" in a causal sense. The world design that depends upon continuity is not a *cause* but the *condition of possibility* for the fantasies, the fears, and the anxiety attacks. He adds that

> the skating incident assumed its traumatic significance because, in it, the world suddenly changed its face, disclosed itself from the angle of suddenness, of something totally different, new, and unexpected. For that there was no place in this child's world; it could not enter into her world-design; it stayed, as it were, always outside; it could not be mastered. (1958a, p. 204)

The world design upon which all these experiences are based "does not have to be 'conscious,' but neither must we call it 'unconscious' in the psychoanalytic sense." That is, it is a *horizon*, as described in Chapter 2.

A second patient suffered all sorts of somatic preoccupations, phobias about what he might do and about what might be done to him. He was diagnosed as a "polymorphous schizophrenic" because of the seemingly bewildering combination of symptoms, most of which led him into remarkably bizarre behavior. Binswanger notes:

> Whereas in our first case everything that is *(alles Seiende)* was only accessible in a world reduced to the category of continuity, in this case it is a world reduced to the mechanical category of push and pressure. We are therefore not surprised to see that in this existence and its world there is no steadiness, that its stream of life does not flow quietly along, but that everything occurs by jerks and starts, from the simplest gestures and movements to the formulation of linguistic expression and the performance of thinking and volitional decisions. Everything about the patient is jagged and occurs abruptly, while between the single jerks and pushes emptiness prevails. (1958a, p. 207)*

*These quotes from Binswanger are reprinted by permission of the publisher from *Existence: A New Dimension in Psychiatry and Psychology,* edited by Rollo May, Ernest Angel, and Henri F. Ellenberger, © 1958 by Basic Books, Inc., Publishers, New York.

A third patient's world was "reduced to the categories of familiarity and strangeness—or uncanniness." This patient "was constantly threatened by a prowling, as yet impersonal, hostile power." These experiences later proliferated in delusions of persecution. As in the other cases, the delusions were not the random events of a deranged mind, but rather they concretely articulated her world. At the same time, her delusions (or any experience) could come about only on the basis of a world design that supplied the basis, the context, the conditions of possibility for these experiences.

Moods and individual life styles are not the only things elucidated by a phenomenological study of world. Consider also situations. Everyone knows that the "atmosphere" is very different at a birthday party, a murder trial, and a funeral—though each can look like either of the other two under certain circumstances. In these settings, we are pulled into a "collective mood," as it were—one that is all the more poignant because of each individual's sensitivity to it and the tendency of us all to contribute to that atmosphere, once caught up in it, by communicating it to others. I know of one phenomenological psychologist who is trying to describe the atmosphere of psychotherapy with different patients in different settings. This effort promises a substantial contribution to the psychotherapeutic literature. Others have explored the "virtual world" of a novel or other piece of art. Literary sensitivity will benefit, and with it we shall all become more attuned to life.

In each of these kinds of studies, the possibilities for a phenomenological psychology are barely glimpsed. In each a new version of "the phenomenological method" will have to be devised, though the general strategies of Chapter 3 remain invaluable guides. Multiple layers of meaning will be sought and described, and their coherence in experiential wholes will become vivid. Lying at the base of all such descriptions will be "worlds" to be appreciated and the "world" to be understood.

CHAPTER
11

CLOSING COMMENTS

I recall a class, in which two professors and ten students who had come to know and like one another, turned their attention to one another as individuals; comments on one another's behavior and style came forth, and we all enjoyed a heightened sense of respect for one another even as we became more candid in our remarks. One student had not read very much of the material, but everyone liked him because of his ability to cheer us up by pointing out our occasional absurdity as we pursued deep philosophical issues. I said something to that effect to him; it was, I am afraid, a rather left-handed compliment, but I meant it. Everyone looked at him, expecting another of his famous comments. He paused, then said: "You better watch out. I might say something really brilliant some day."

It was funny, but also serious. The remark was a response to the friendly atmosphere of the proceedings with a characteristically unexpected theme. The student managed, first, to maintain his posture of good-natured levity; second, to acknowledge that he had not said anything brilliant so far; third, to make a joke about how he would be in the future; and, fourth, to demand respect for the person he was, even though he was different from the rest of us.

The moment passed with a good laugh, but it deserves to be preserved as an example of how creative human behavior can be. Had he taken the time to think of something to say that would have achieved all those ends; had he sorted out the various meanings of what was happening in the room, what was said to him, and what it meant for everyone to look at him expectantly;

had he recalled all the feelings he had had toward the course and the people there; and had he planned what kind of relationships he wanted to have in the future, he could not have come up with a better comment. Indeed, his spontaneous reaction combined all these motives, meanings, memories, and plans in an instant. That is how behavior usually is. We really ought to see it in its full complexity and abundance of meaning if we want to understand it.

We began Part I with a phenomenological analysis of my daughter's changing her mind one night. We have come back to that episode many times, from many different angles, seeking to unpack its meanings in their full richness and complexity. The amazing thing is that this episode has so many meanings. But it is no more amazing than any other episode involving you or me five minutes ago or tomorrow. Most of our behavior is at least as complex, and most of us already understand it in its complexity, though not explicitly. Nothing is too trivial for a phenomenological analysis, for everything we do engages all the levels and layers of who we are.

Behavior is an expression of who we are at the moment, have been, and will be in the long run; it is also a response to a physiognomic field that is in constant flux, but with a pattern; it also enacts our part in multiple interpersonal agreements, past, present, and future. Behavior is making public who we are; it may emanate from a private nexus of secret thoughts and feelings, but our privacy does not and cannot remain all that private. A person may deceive us for a short time, but a long-term deception is so rare that we always count it as a remarkable event, not because we are trained phenomenologists but because we are untrained phenomenologists who already understand more than we know about ourselves and one another. But, as long as this understanding remains implicit and not subject to rigorous scrutiny, we are likely to cover it up with flashy but simple theories that ignore life as we really live it.

We of our species are indeed capable of ignoring life as we really live it. But we are also capable, unlike any other species, of paying explicit attention to behavior in its richness and complexity. An adequate psychology is one that opens us to ourselves, our lived experience, instead of covering experience up with global explanations according to which everything means the same thing.

But psychology is an extremely young science. Phenomenological psychology is even younger. If you have taken my advice in the Preface and have attempted to do some analytic work as you went along, you have probably discovered that understanding behavior is not as easy as many of the examples have made it seem. There is, first of all, the task of being open to one's own experience. This openness requires a most extraordinary discipline because we have learned, over years of training, to ignore so much of our experience. What does it feel like to be in such and such a situation? Most situations are "processed" by us with a kind of intellectual efficiency that closes us to seeing clearly what we already understand, and must understand in order to be counted among the sane in our culture. Most of us on this planet will find our way to our graves without ever coming to terms with life itself. That is sad, to be sure, but it is far from necessary. As human beings, we have not only the remarkable ability to synthesize horizons into experience and to articulate experience into behavior at the drop of a hat; we also have the even more remarkable ability to come to know *what* we are doing, *why*, and with *what effect*—but only if we try to go beyond those stereotyped meanings so glibly offered by our culture, only if we can discipline ourselves into a reflective and critical posture, only if we are curious.

A second difficulty, once we are in more vivid touch with our lived experience, is how to articulate what we find there. This problem is largely one of language. We may say that our work in Part III has been primarily to establish a language: some descriptive terms with which to work and some approaches to relating these terms to one another conceptually without doing violence to the data of lived experience.[1] Again, the extreme youth of our science shows itself. There are potentially an infinite number of ways to isolate and label the various levels of meaning in human experience; not all of them are equally useful, accurate, or revealing of life as we live it. These criteria can be found nowhere else than in lived experience; our enterprise becomes naturally circular in this sense. But it is not free-floating, groundless, without basis. Nor can its description be arbitrary or merely a matter of taste. Psychological theory must be grounded in the only place that any meaning at all can be grounded: everyday experience. If concepts like the world, physiognomy, guilt, collusion, and so on do not speak to our experience or if they obscure enduring and important experiential differences, they will have to be revised.

Some of the difficulties, but by no means all of them, can be alleviated by psychology itself, which is a body of literature and a program for creating more literature. As students of psychology we have a right to exploit the existing literature so that we may become more transparent to ourselves, and we have the obligation to create more and better literature for our children.

PHENOMENOLOGICAL AND OTHER PSYCHOLOGIES[2]

It is probably an error to divide various psychologies too sharply between those that seek to predict, or control, behavior and those that seek to understand people. Most psychologists seek to do both. Phenomenological psychology is at one extreme of such a continuum in that it does not seek to predict or control behavior, and focuses exclusively on the task of under-understanding. There are extreme psychologies in the other direction, for example, that of B. F. Skinner (1953, 1972). (Curiously, Skinnerians and phenomenologists have significant common ground, often standing against the rest of the discipline.[3]) The phenomenological argument is that, if we want to understand people, we must approach the task with methods and with concepts that are exclusively geared to that task. To the extent that modern psychology has borrowed methods and concepts from physics, it is limited to understanding only those features of man that are shared with physical objects. To the extent that it has borrowed methods and concepts from biology, it is limited to understanding those features of man that are shared with organisms in general. Phenomenological psychology seeks to understand people as people; that is one of the reasons why it focuses on experience.

There are other psychologies that seek to understand people as people, like so-called humanist psychology or personology.[4] Like phenomenological psychology, personology recognizes that people do have things in common with physical objects and with organisms in general. These other kinds of psychology are therefore not worthless in our attempt to understand people. But like Willie Sutton, who said he robbed banks "because that's where the money is," phenomenologists and personologists seek a more direct approach. If we want to understand people, then we should study people, and we should devise concepts and methods appropriate *for that study.* It is obvious that phenomenological psychologists attempt to go farther than the personologists in that program.

Psychologists do not ask very often why we want to have a psychology at all, what we mean when we say we "understand" something, and what is at stake in communicating our understanding. Because phenomenological psychology emerges from a philosophical tradition different from the physical and biological sciences, its answers to these questions are often different from those of mainstream American psychology. Phenomenological psychology stands or falls on its own merit as a kind of psychology, however, and does not depend on association with impressive and renowned philosophers.

Not that this kind of psychology is not indebted to Edmund Husserl, Martin Heidegger, Jean-Paul Sartre, and Maurice Merleau-Ponty. It is most assuredly more their creation than mine. It also does not mean that we can dispense with these thinkers in the pursuit of a phenomenological psychology, especially in its most basic philosophical starting points. But it does mean that it is possible for beginning students to think phenomenologically, to do phenomenology, and certainly to understand what psychology tries to understand in an incisive and penetrating way.

Even though phenomenological psychology is valuable because it confronts us with basic questions not usually asked and leads us to explore issues with the philosophers, its most basic value is to open our eyes and our minds to lived experience. That is also its most basic task. Indeed, that recommendation sums up the work of all phenomenologists. I have tried, with uneven success I am sure, to further progress on that task with this book. If we are not open to the lived experience of the world, we shall have a strange psychology indeed. Naturally, working with "the subjective" and with unique events causes problems—some say insurmountable problems. That is an exaggeration.

It is probably significant that phenomenological psychology appears at a certain time in our cultural history. Although it fits neatly into current reservations about science and technology, it must stand or fall on its own merits and not on its association with popular antitechnological sentiments.[5]

We must avoid promising too much. I do firmly believe that a phenomenological approach to psychology relieves our discipline's most basic problems with moral issues[6] by adopting an appreciative, instead of a manipulative, attitude and by incorporating that attitude into its very fiber. But it is far from clear that this kind of psychology will ever be anything more than a minority voice or that it will ever appear to be adequate in a culture that defines adequacy in technological terms.

Nevertheless, I write this book with a hope: that we can as a culture, as a discipline and profession, and as individuals come to recognize that the phenomena we study mean many things, that we can come to understand the many layers and nuances of meaning inherent in human behavior. Phenomenological psychology is nothing more than making explicit and rigorous our everyday experience. It is no more desirable than everyday experience is important. But, because all knowledge has meaning only in relation to life as it is lived by people every day, this importance and desirability are absolute.

APPENDIX

FOR PSYCHOLOGISTS ONLY: THE PLACE OF PHENOMENOLOGICAL PSYCHOLOGY

In 1890 William James first defined psychology for Americans. It was to be the science of mental life: And with the idea that there should be such a science, backed by James' scholarship, goodwill, and vision, our people were given a whole new outlook on themselves. At first, only a handful of scholars understood what psychology was, but their diligent efforts to establish the new science eventually yielded, in a few short decades, a new center of gravity for undergraduate studies and a new way for Americans to think about themselves. Americans by the millions became something few men before had been: willing objects of a new science, a new science in which they themselves—we ourselves—could also be the scientists. Ours is a century in which human self-consciousness has taken a unique and pervasive turn, and the advent of American psychology was one of the causes of that turn in the mental life that psychology itself studies.

James consolidated and Americanized little pieces of psychological self-consciousness as it had developed in Europe and England. He gave it a scope that excluded nothing that we are, from the tiniest detail of our brain and the most secret thought about ourselves to the largest and most public events perpetrated by men. The very notion of psychology exposed the whole range of who we are for our own scrutiny. The birth of American psychology with James' *Principles of Psychology* led to astounding twists and turns in our definitions of ourselves. There have been continuities beneath discontinuities beneath continuities—the history of psychology is already so complex that to teach a course, for example, on that history offers as many possibilities as does one's personal self-definition. Some say the science is in its infancy, others that it is adolescent, still others that it is mature. Just what we say of psychology's progress to date depends on what we envision James to have borne.

Early in its development American psychology was very much in the business of importing. The thinking of Wilhelm Wundt was imported from Germany to E. B. Titchener's Cornell University, Ivan Pavlov from Russia to John Watson's Columbia University, and Alfred Binet from France to Stanford University, but in each instance the import was Americanized. Later came Sigmund Freud and *Gestalt* psychology, against the backdrop of Charles Darwin, who had wrenched England and the United States in the last century, and of James, who had prepared us for these imports by inventing a new American for psychology—a new "man" as object of psychological self-consciousness. No one quite knew, or knows, where psychology is going. *That* it is going on and on, however, seems a safe prediction for the foreseeable future.

Phenomenological psychology is another in the list of imports from Europe. Like former imports, it already had precursors in this or that corner of home-grown American psychology. And also like former imports, it is destined to be Americanized, even as it will enrich the American self-consciousness that will incorporate it. The precise nature of that enrichment is, at this point, quite unclear. How it will actually work out in the chaotic marketplace of ideas remains a question. But it is perhaps important to note that phenomenological psychologists have some vision of this future. We must state our intentions and share our hopes openly with the established authorities of American psychological self-consciousness, academic psychologists. Every new idea is, in some sense, a threat to old ideas, and the history of psychology in this country is a fascinating tale of negotiations among men about what will be the language of our self-understanding.

More specifically, just what do we think the contribution of phenomenology to the rich conglomeration of ideas that now characterizes American academic psychology can be? It seems to me that there are four levels at which phenomenology will enter this matrix, and I want, in this brief essay, to try to describe the ways that phenomenology can make a contribution.

SOURCE OF HYPOTHESES

Through its natural-science methodology, psychology has been, for some decades now, in the business of verifying hypotheses. Where do these hypotheses come from? From hunches, intuitions, educated guesses, and the creative reading of previous findings. The most innovative developments in psychology have been the products of psychologists who have looked at phenomena they wanted to understand, then looked again and then again, asking such questions as "What would have to be true for *that* to happen?" Not infrequently psychologists use their own experience as a source of hunches. "How would I react if I were in this situation?"

All these processes, which are never included in official accounts of psychological methodology, are phenomenological in an informal and non-systematic sense. Phenomenological reductions, imaginative variations, and interpretations have always been the stock in trade of creative scientists, but they have not been spelled out in detail as methodological procedures. Before phenomenology they had also not been made rigorous or systematic. At the simplest level of its contribution, phenomenology can offer a clear description of, and some systematic rigor in, this crucial but usually ne-glected stage of the scientific process.

More specifically, the concern of phenomenology is experience. Because experience plays a part in nearly all behavior, the findings of phenomenolo-gists can fit into the already-existing paradigm of scientific psychology as a source of "intervening variables." An intervening variable is a presumed event that occurs inside the organism, between a stimulus input and a response output. Such "internal" processes are not directly visible and are thus not amenable to conventional science, yet they are probably critical parts of the production of behavior. *Experience* is precisely such an "inter-vening variable" when it is seen from the point of view of natural science.

Most psychologists have hypothesized intervening variables to explain the observable relations between stimuli going into and responses coming out of an organism. Those of learning theorist Clark Hull (1952) are almost pure logical inferences, and therefore they are not particularly phenomenological. In contrast, those of learning theorist E. C. Tolman (1966) are highly phe-nomenological in content, and Tolman's method was openly to ask "How would I behave if I were in this situation?" Fritz Heider's book *The Psy-chology of Interpersonal Relations* (1958) represents an elaborate attempt to understand experience as it is experienced, and nearly every chapter has given birth to a subfield of contemporary social psychology. The *Gestalt* psychologists were clearly inspired by some peculiarities of subjective experience to create some of our most exciting psychological literature. Kurt Lewin (1935) must be mentioned in this connection as well. Of course, Snygg and Combs (1949) and MacLeod advertised themselves as phenomenologists and provoked many hypotheses.

None of these psychologists was a phenomenologist in the rather strict sense that phenomenologists now use that term, yet they were all phenomenological at that crucial point at which they "understood" behavior: before demonstrating it experimentally. Naturally, hunches that emerge from a nonsystematic and informal phenomenological speculation are not always correct in the sense of the "correctness" of natural science. This sort of "phenomenology" therefore needs a scientific method of verification. But, at the same time, science needs this sort of phenomenology as a source of hypotheses. It needs phenomenology not only to provide creative new slants on old problems but also to provide theoretical content related to how people actually live. A well-developed phenomenological psychology will provide scientific psychologists, who prefer to cast their work in the mold of experimental science, with theoretical ideas about how people actually live, thus helping to make their experimental work more incisive, relevant, and useful.

Let me offer an even more specific example of what I mean, though the work of any of the psychologists mentioned is full of such examples. Suppose that we want to know what kinds of factors determine interpersonal attraction. Research on this subject has shown that we can predict how much a subject will be attracted to a person by knowing some of the subject's characteristics, his personality traits and so on. We can also predict with some accuracy on the basis of the characteristics of the person to who whom he is attracted. That is, some people are more attractive than others. Putting these two kinds of information together, we can predict any individual attraction with more accuracy than if we knew only one of these predictors. But there is yet another variable that influences the degree of attraction in any particular instance, and that is the situation within which two people meet (Frankel, 1973). Subject A meeting person B will not feel the same attraction in a bar, in church, in the woods, and in an orgy. If the subject sees the situation as scary, challenging, comfortable, tense, or the like, the degree of his attraction will be affected. But what are the situational features that make a difference? How the subject perceives the situation will matter, but how can we know *what* it is he perceives in a situation that matters? What are the "dimensions" of situations? That is, what are the "prototypical situations"?

Does our list of "scary," "challenging," and so on discriminate the relevant situational differences? What is needed is a phenomenology of situations to give the experimenter an idea of how to vary them in testing his predictions.

A VEHICLE FOR HUMANISM

Natural science is largely centered around a method and is independent of other traditions of Western thought that are fruitful for psychology. Humanism is such a tradition. By "humanism," I mean simply that line of thought that begins with the premise that we must understand *people* in terms that are appropriate to people, rather than in terms borrowed from physics or biology. This tradition is not equally relevant or useful for all branches of psychology, but it is certainly relevant for clinical psychology and the study of personality, "abnormal" behavior, and so on. It is in these fields that humanism has had a presence in psychology, through the work of Carl Rogers, Gordon Allport, Rollo May, George Kelly, Clark Moustakas, Abraham Maslow, Sidney Jourard, and many others.

A humanistic point of view places consciousness in the center of the concept of man, for consciousness dominates the life of man more dramatically than perhaps any other organism. His behavior is less mechanical, less predictable, less a direct function of the environment, and more dependent on how he sees the world in general and his immediate situation in particular.

By focusing on a patient's experience, as well as on his behavior, psychologists are being both phenomenological and humanistic. A well-developed phenomenological psychology will provide a theory of what it is like to be a person (rather than a thing or an organism). Such a theory will enable the humanistic tradition to have a more coherent and rigorous presence in American psychology.

The humanistic concern for people as experiencing beings is already the common ground of humanistic and phenomenological psychologists. They contribute to each other, but humanism today, though obviously influential in clinical psychology, lacks a method, a coherent theory, and an explicit grounding in rigorous data. Humanistic goals (understanding and helping people) are manifestly different from scientific goals (prediction and control), but humanistic psychology today seems more like a moral concern pasted onto scientific psychology for its clinical applications than a distinguishable program.

In its clinical applications, psychology cannot simply superimpose a natural-science framework on the clinical task without leaving something out. Attempts like B. F. Skinner's effort to solve human problems technologically create profound discomfort among humanists, but this discomfort is more usually articulated as moral qualms than as intellectual challenge.

The latter needs to be developed to give more substance to the former. Phenomenological psychology can thus be an intellectual vehicle for the humanistic response to technologies like those of Skinner through further development of the theory of man as an experiencing being. If humanists want to argue that we must understand experience in order to understand patients, then it is necessary actually to understand experience instead of merely to make the argument. To offer a coherent understanding is necessary to make the argument cogent. Phenomenological psychology holds forth this promise.

A PARADIGM

Thomas Kuhn (1962), in his study of scientific revolutions, has isolated a level of science that he calls "paradigm." A paradigm is a complex of assumptions, of ways of seeing and thinking, that lies beneath theories and models. In its evolution, science may discover a number of facts without changing theories, but theories do ultimately evolve as the result of facts. Similarly, a number of theories or models may come into focus without a paradigm shift, but at crucial points in the history of science paradigms do change. Such changes in paradigms ("revolutions") not only change the perception of facts and theories in such a way that some of those that did not seem important before now become important. Paradigm shifts also redefine useful knowledge, the kinds of questions asked, the criteria for what will be called answers, and in some senses the goals of the science.

American psychology experienced such a dramatic revolution between the years 1915 and 1930, when the very goals of psychology changed from a quest for the elemental atoms of mind (Titchener's "structuralism") to a search for the laws and principles that would enable psychologists to predict and control behavior (Watson's "behaviorism"). Other innovations in psychology—by Freud, Jean Piaget, Gestalt psychologists, neuropsychologist D. O. Hebb, cognitive psychologists (in studies of information processing), ethologists, and Skinner (operant technology)—have been nearly as radical, at least in intent, but they have not in fact been as pervasive and "revolutionary" as Watson's behaviorism was. Watson's concept provoked a genuine paradigm shift; the psychologists mentioned have certainly disagreed with Watson's theory but have operated largely within his paradigm. Since Watson participants in American mainstream psychology have agreed that it is important to understand only those psychological factors that affect *behavior,* the definition of understanding has been the ability to predict and control *behavior.*

Phenomenological psychology, in its more ambitious moments, seeks to establish a new paradigm for psychology. This new paradigm will involve a change in which facts and theories are important: what questions to ask, what qualifies as an answer, and, in general, the goals of the science.

Now, the situation in American psychology today is so pluralistic that a sweeping paradigm shift of the magnitude of Watson's shift is probably not possible. Psychologists would never agree on what to shift *to* when there are already profound disagreements about what we would be shifting *from.* Therefore, the more modest presence of phenomenological psychology, described as "a source of hypotheses" and "a vehicle for humanism," is a more likely historical prediction. In order for even these kinds of influences to come to fruition, however, we must suppose a fuller development of phenomenological psychology than now exists. This development, in turn, will rely on a fuller development of a paradigm—an elaboration of the important questions and the development of a method for answering them. Because phenomenological psychologists are not satisfied with the current preparadigmatic status of their work, a paradigm will develop as different from current mainstream psychology as Watson's paradigm was from Titchener's structuralism. The ultimate fate of that paradigm and the psychological understanding that emerges from it will be questions for future generations of psychologists.

From the point of view of a phenomenological paradigm, predicting and controlling behavior are not particularly important goals, nor are they criteria of knowledge; a phenomenologist would not agree that we "know" or "understand" something only when we can predict and control it. Verification of knowledge will probably be more akin to an agreement based on the fact that the knowledge is already how we understand ourselves. That is, we do already understand ourselves in some particular ways, and that self-understanding is a part of how we indeed are.

Let me try to elaborate this difficult but crucial point. In the course of a day, I behave all day. Psychology offers me concepts in terms of which I can understand my own behavior. It is, for example, a sequence of responses to a sequence of stimuli or a discharge of psychodynamic energy channeled through a network of ego-defense mechanisms. These theories are part of how I (and all other Americans) understand myself. I also understand myself, however, as striving for a particular future or avoiding one, as indulging preferences, fulfilling obligations, proving something to someone, resisting temptations, demonstrating courage, affirming my rights, and so on. None of this language is the language of psychological theory, yet it is the fabric of my nontheoretical self-understanding. In order to bring my psychological theory to bear, I must translate these terms into psychological ones.

Such a translation is clearly reductionist, but we are happy to pay that price in order to have a science. The alternative to such reduction has always seemed to be mere stream-of-consciousness reporting—poetry, literature, inspiration, or confession, but not psychology. The phenomenological paradigm rests on the assumption that this level of everyday, nontheoretical self-understanding can be the subject matter of psychology, because it is not random, orderless, or unstructured. The task is merely to find a way to articulate that already existing order and structure explicitly. Phenomenological psychology will thus seek to make clear how we are as living and experiencing people. We have not achieved this understanding because psychology has not had that goal or the theory and language in which to achieve it. And, when we do achieve it, it will reveal ourselves to ourselves in such a way that we will know that it is true.

If this promise sounds like magic, it is partly because we are accustomed to testing knowledge by the old paradigm. But the old paradigm did not address the question of how we actually live our experience, and indeed it could not do so with its method. Even more important, however, we must note that our understanding of what it means to be a human being already enjoys striking agreement. But, because it has not been articulated, it has remained at the level of an unexamined assumption. Phenomenological psychology will articulate this level of our experience. It will make clear our now foggy understanding that we are who and how we are only on the basis of there being a world and, furthermore, a world with such and such a character, shared with others, extended in space, and changing with time. All this complexity constitutes a frame of meaning within which we interpret our everyday experience. And these meanings are available for scrutiny and criticism—but only after a paradigm has been developed.

The phenomenological paradigm will seek to reveal ourselves to ourselves. It will tell us what we already know and how we already live, rather than pushing back frontiers of new knowledge after the fashion of the physical sciences. But, even though we already know what it will tell us, we do not know *that* we know it. We do not have a clear and articulate understanding of who and how we are who we are, and therefore we do not see, except vaguely and unsystematically, what our options are. Perhaps M. Foucault (1970) was right when he suggested that "man" (as we know him) was invented in the late eighteenth century and that we are approaching a time when "he" will disappear and a new understanding of ourselves will emerge.

A RESPONSE TO CRISIS

Psychologists have frequently understood their science as practical, addressing social problems and nudging the course of history toward a more reasonable and humane way of life. The striking social and political disasters of this centruy have occurred against the backdrop of psychological self-consciousness, and Americans have had a sense that they can intervene intelligently to make life better. Even though this century may offer no more severe "crises" than previous ones, they seem more severe because we feel more able to respond intelligently. Skinner's behavioral technology (1970) is only the most obvious example of this attitude.

From its very inception in the early work of Husserl, phenomenology was also seen by its author as a response to a peculiarly modern crisis. Husserl himself was not very articulate about that crisis until the end of his life, in his posthumous book, *The Crisis of European Sciences and Transcendental Phenomenology* (1970). His particular understanding of the crisis is based on the broad outlines and assumptions of modern thought since the sixteenth century. Martin Heidegger's somewhat different reading (1962) of our situation suggests a 2000-year mistake. Other phenomenologists see it yet differently.

In general, phenomenologists understand the crisis to be deeper and more complex than do other American psychologists. They share none of Skinner's technological optimism, but they also by-pass the psychologist's notion that aggression is merely innate. They tend to tap human history at the level of the assumptions basic to traditions and the collective consciousness of society. This approach has led to a variety of interpretations that may well seem speculative and irrelevant to the more practical style of American psychologists, even in their attempts to meet the crisis.

But some of these very profound historical assumptions are directly relevant to psychologists. Most obviously, our traditions have put us in the peculiar situation in which facts and values are radically split from each other.

This split between facts and values in modern thought has an immediate pinch for psychologists in the application of their science to human affairs. Who is mentally ill? What is mental health? What are the costs of human conformity? How can they be balanced against the dangers of behavioral deviance? Are these "value questions" forever outside the scope of our science? How can they possibly be separated without splitting ourselves as psychologists? How can they possibly be related systematically to one another, given an intellectual tradition that insists that they are separate? Can we free ourselves from this traditional split, which totally pervades our very language and thought? Or are we condemned to develop a more and more refined technology for achieving ends, leaving the question of the ends themselves to be decided as matters of taste, political power, and historical accident?

I have already taken up the question of the contribution of phenomenology to psychology at this level in another work (Keen, 1972), and I shall not repeat that here. It is important to note, however, that phenomenology has a presence on this level of a cultural movement or tradition in the history of ideas, as well as at the levels of paradigm, the theory of human experiencing, and a source of natural scientific hypotheses.

DOING PSYCHOLOGY PHENOMENOLOGICALLY

Because his psychology is still largely preparadigmatic, the phenomenological psychologist experiences some pain and embarrassment when a colleague asks him quite simply "What do you do?" In part, what we do depends upon which of our four levels of application we are interested in. Yet each level depends, as already noted, upon the development of a clearer and more communicable paradigm. I think an attempt must be made, even at this early stage, to answer the question.

The goal of phenomenological psychology is to reveal—for our explicit understanding—ourselves to ourselves. We must do that by observing ourselves and one another. Such observation, of self and others, may be taken roughly to correspond to introspective and behavioral methodologies respectively. Phenomenological work is limited to neither of these two but presupposes both, depends on them, and uses them. Beyond observing ourselves and others, phenomenological work involves disciplined reflection upon our own observation. Naturally, good scientists have always reflected, but it has never become a method with a goal of its own, questions of its own, answers of its own, and an orderly procedure for moving from one to the other.

More particularly, the goal of phenomenological psychology is to reveal for our explicit understanding those things that we already implicitly understand. As mentioned earlier, our everyday, living understanding of ourselves is not exhausted by our psychological theories. Every time I have a conversation with another person, for example, I understand what I say from his point of view (that is how I know *what* to say), and I know implicitly that he does the same with respect to me. Together we establish an intricate network of agreements, not only about what our linguistic utterances will refer to, but also about which ones are proper to utter, in what circumstances, for what reasons, and so on. Or, more precisely and very importantly, we do not *establish* these agreements, for they are already there. They are part of the fabric of our lives and of the lives of everyone who has ever had a conversation at all. Can these agreements be specified? Is it necessary or rewarding to do so? How can we approach this task?

Agreements can be specified, but only if we inquire after them through disciplined reflection. It is not necessary to do so in order to get along in the everyday world, but it is necessary in order to understand *how* we get along in the everyday world—or how we fail to do so. It is desirable to inquire only to the degree that it is desirable to have such understanding. Phenomenologists share that value with many nonphenomenologists, but it is clearly not shared by psychologists who orient their work toward the exclusive goals of prediction and control of behavior.

Disciplined reflection itself is not easy to describe, and, of course, that is the paradigmatic problem. It probably cannot be reduced to "cookbook" instructions. To return to our example of a conversation, how do we know what our utterances sound like and mean to others? Of course, we sometimes err in this judgment, and that impresses us, but disciplined reflection leads us to see how remarkable is the ordinarily unimpressive fact that we do it so well.

How do we do it? Somehow, our experience of ourselves in conversation with others has some *given* qualities that have not been very intensely investigated. I locate the other in a physical space that is understood to be within the range of my voice, and I know he does the same to me. But I also locate myself and the other in a kind of psychological space in which we are transparent to one another. In my everyday conversations, I assume that the contents of my experience are communicable to him and his to me, that we share an intention to reveal ourselves to each other, that this intention fits into a psychological (or experiential) space of my larger life that is different from but overlaps his, that this overlap contains a shared concept of the world, that that world also looks different from the two perspectives, that I can lead him to understand my perspective (within limits), and that I can understand his—if we agree to try. Even if we do not agree to try, we shall inevitably understand each other to a remarkable degree. How is it that we understand so much? Because that is the character of human experience. Experience is not ephemeral and ineffable; it is minutely structured according to a space in which we already know that a shared physical space will be a shared experiential space, but with unique features according to our differing perspectives. I am not alone in the world and have never assumed that I am. Insofar as human experience is truly human, it has that character.

Developmentally speaking, the acquisition of this interpersonal character of experience probably occurs very early, though we know from the work of Piaget that it probably undergoes an orderly development from the earliest empathic feeling of rapport with the mother to the sophisticated abilities to lie and to anticipate others' conclusions, as well as other trappings of everyday experience as adults. Fascinating as the developmental question is, my own preference is to understand first the experiential structures in which development occurs—and here I find, as a phenomenologist, that the limitation of Piaget's investigation to logical thought, which is one but not the only structure of experience, does not offer a very full phenomenological psychology. The structures of human experience that make my everyday life possible are much more elaborate than formal operations—even if we throw in perseverations from concrete operations and preoperational cognition. The work of Freud, H. S. Sullivan, and George Kelly is also suggestive.

These theories seem more incomplete than wrong. Each of them contributes a part, but the whole is more than the sum of the parts, at least as far as experience is concerned. And to go beyond this statement to the characterization that appears in phenomenological theory goes beyond our purpose here. Our point here is simply that such investigations need not be groundless, beyond agreement, and out of sight of psychology; phenomenologists are working to specify the paradigm that can bring it all into focus.

CONCLUSION

So what is the "place" of phenomenological psychology amid the complex network of ideas that constitutes American academic psychology? Each of the levels we have discussed has been more ambitious, more far-reaching, more visionary than the previous one. The first level can be predicted confidently, for it is an already established fact of history. But operation on that level will expand and become more important as phenomenological psychology itself develops. The second-level operation is already apparent in some senses, but it too depends on the continuing development of the work itself. The third level, the paradigm, will come to pass. The question of its importance for psychology is probably not for the current generation of psychologists to decide. The fourth level is one about which only fools make predictions, but we may hope that, as a way of thinking, phenomenology will contribute to an escape from our cultural crisis—if there is a crisis and if we are to escape it.

I find myself wondering what the William James of 1890 would say about academic psychology today. The many inconsistencies and contradictions in James' own psychology are still with us. We see them somewhat differently today, but they are, in all likelihood, not merely contradictions in psychological theory; rather, they are contradictions in Western thought in general—perhaps even paradoxes in human existence itself. Husserl was apparently more impressed with James than the reverse, but phenomenology has come a long way, as has psychology, since either of them wrote their seminal works. Now is an exciting time, when successors of both men speak to one another from the vantage point of that peculiar American self-consciousness that is academic psychology.

NOTES

CHAPTER 1

[1] One of the few psychological studies of this question is by E. T. Gendlin (1962).

[2] There have been very few phenomenological studies of children. The work of Maurice Merleau-Ponty (1964a) is a notable exception. The most salient and sagacious psychologist specializing in children is probably Jean Piaget, who is often phenomenological in method and content, though not explicitly so. A good source book on Piaget's voluminous work is J. H. Flavell (1963). A critique of Piaget's work from a phenomenological point of view can be found in B. Levi (1972). For Piaget's own view of phenomenology and other philosophical enterprises, see Piaget (1971).

[3] A number of psychologists have differentiated shame from guilt in precisely this way (for example, Lynd, 1961). One can feel guilty alone; it is a matter of self-judgment. On the other hand, the real, imagined, or implicit presence of others is an inherent part of the experience of shame; the other is the judge and the self is the judged. Considered developmentally, guilt probably derives from shame; the child is sensitive to parental disapproval before he learns to disapprove of himself. Even mature guilt probably always has something of shame in it, so that I feel guilty also because I know important others would judge me badly.

Such distinctions and descriptions are an important part of phenomenological psychology. They help to make clear the structural character of everyday experience. "Structure" refers in this instance to the implicit spatial prerequisite for the experience: Shame occurs in an interpersonal space. The stacking up of temporal backdrops is also an example of structure. Experience is always structured; space and time are two (but not the only two) structures that characterize human experience.

⁴This social character is a third universal aspect of human experience. The physiognomy of physical *space* (as in Figure 5), the structure of *temporal* backdrops (as in Figures 1 and 2), and the structure of *social* relations (as in Figures 3 and 4) are the three "universal horizons" to be discussed in detail in Chapters 7–9 respectively. As will become clear later, there is nothing sacred about these three, and indeed in experience itself, they do not occur as separate issues.

⁵It may be worthwhile to take up here an issue raised by a student when he finished reading Chapter 1. "I read it. I understand what you say; but I still don't know *why* she changed her mind. In spite of all you've said, I still don't think you've explained it so that I can say that I understand it—*really* understand it." This kind of response comes from very thoughtful students. My usual reaction is to ask what *sort* of explanation seems to be missing, what *kinds* of things we would need to know in order *really* to understand why she changed her mind?

We come here, for the first time in this book, face to face with a difficult philosophical issue: What is understanding? The student mentioned had some sense of when he understood something. Generally, it involved knowing a pattern or sequence of antecedent events that caused the event in question. "*Why* did she change her mind?" meant to this student "What caused her to change her mind as she did?" The student is, of course, quite right that there is no answer to that question in this chapter. And he is also correct in saying that the chapter really does not explain anything; it does not explain anything to anyone for whom "understanding" means knowing what causes an event to happen.

If it rains and we want to know *why* it is raining, we shall probably be satisfied that we *understand* why it is raining when we understand the physics of water condensation and temperature patterns and how they apply to today's rain. Why is it raining? The answer lies in a pattern of antecedent events that, when they occur, will always produce rain. When we know the meteorology, then we understand. By this sense of when we understand things, Chapter 1 does not tell us *why* my daughter changed her mind.

Causality is how I understand some things, but it is not how I understand all things. It is not how I understand what the student means even as he expresses his criticism to me. My understanding of people is not analogous to my understanding of the weather. I do not reckon his objection to be the *effect* of a pattern of *causes,* like a scientific background and a reading of the chapter. I grasp what he is saying by *knowing what he means,* not knowing what caused that behavior to emerge from him at this time. He knows what I mean by this statement, and we may say that we "understand" each other.

It is tempting to state flatly that the two kinds of understanding are fundamentally different and that phenomenology aims at the latter, instead of the former, whereas traditional psychology aims at the former. This polarity is temporarily helpful, perhaps, but it is rather too simple, as we shall show in Part II.

[6] This statement implies that there is nothing about ourselves that we do not already know (though we may not know *that* we know it). Such a statement flies in the face of all kinds of facts about the human body and mind that many people never have known and never will know. Yet, if these facts are relevant to their lives and are factors in their behavior, people must know them on some level, in order to behave as they do. This dilemma can be resolved by distinguishing between explicit and implicit knowledge, the latter extending down into organic processes of which we are not aware (as reflected in the statement "My stomach knows when to digest food"). Such a solution is built upon a root metaphor for understanding the body that is very different from the predominant mechanistic metaphor of modern medicine. We cannot argue this issue of the philosophies of science and knowledge here, except to agree that phenomenological psychology challenges some basic assumptions of some scientific thought and throws them into question. This entire issue will appear again in connection with unconscious mental processes in Chapter 2.

CHAPTER 2

[1] This statement is, of course, arguable. In the early decades of this century psychologists dealt with practically nothing but conscious experience. Their psychology was largely frustrating because of their doctrinaire arguments about which building blocks of consciousness are really fundamental. The predominant doctrines were, first, British empiricism, which argued that consciousness must be understood in terms of the elemental parts of its *content*—sensations, images, and affects—and, second, the German protophenomenology of F. Brentano and the Würzburg school, which argues that *acts*, not contents, are the stuff of which consciousness is made (see Brentano, 1874, and Titchener, 1966, for primary statements; good secondary sources are Boring, 1950, and Heidbreder, 1933). The frustrating thing was that there seemed to be no way to resolve this controversy, which involved very different conceptions of the nature of man and how we know him.

In this country, John Watson (1924), the most famous of the behaviorists, solved the problem by redefining psychology in such a way that conscious experience was *not* a part of it. Although this view was opposed by Gestalt psychologists (Koffka, 1935; Köhler, 1947) and others, behaviorism has been the major force in American psychology. Its latest and clearest spokesman is B. F. Skinner (1953, 1972); nevertheless, many psychologists who disagree with Skinner still maintain that psychology can proceed without reference to conscious experience.

The predominant opinion in this country today is probably something like the following: "Conscious experience may play an important role in some behavior, but it cannot be investigated directly because it is subjective, private, and not available to the methods of objective science. Everything we know about conscious experience is therefore indirect—an inference from behavior. And, because experiments, predictions, and other routines of natural science are proceeding without direct exploration of experience, the loss must not be too great." This view is debatable at every point. For a fuller discussion, see A. Giorgi (1966, 1970a, 1970b), J. A. Beshai (1971), S. Strasser (1963), Merleau-Ponty (1964c), and the appendix to this book.

One exception to this predominant view deems awareness important in that subjects' awareness affects how they are conditioned (Grings, 1973). This view is not really that different from Watson and Skinner's assumption, for awareness becomes merely another variable in the laboratory and not a phenomenon in its own right, worthwhile as a focus of study.

Meanwhile, a less prominent but important segment of opinion about the role of experience in psychology is represented by attribution theorists (Jones *et al.*, 1972). Attributionists describe the theory as a modest part of a larger study of how people see the world. Their particular contribution is to pull into focus the *causal* perceptions of our everyday experience. Such causal perceptions are present, they argue, because men have a reality-and-control orientation. But there are also other orientations. Dissonance theory (Festinger, 1957), consistency theories (Abelson *et al.*, 1968), and expectancy theories (Rotter, 1966) exist side by side with attribution theory. Each describes an aspect of the experience of man.

The task of describing experience as a whole, within which each of these theories can assume a special expertise, remains to be done. In times past, Gestalt psychologists approached this task; Kurt Lewin (1935, 1936) and Fritz Heider (1958) made many valuable suggestions that could bear on that task. However, the feeling among current workers in these fields seems to be that a general theory is premature, beyond us at this time. Phenomenologists, on the other hand, prefer to work from experience as a whole to its specifiable parts, each of which would have an already clear context and place in the whole by virtue of the general picture with which they begin. They would dislike, therefore, this statement by the attribution theorists: "The 'meaning' of the event and [one's] subsequent reaction to it are determined to an important degree by its assigned cause" (Jones *et al.*,

1972, p. xi). To a phenomenologist, this statement is exactly backward; the "meaning" is the larger, contextual, and prior factor; the "assigned cause" is derivative. This difference in style, between atomists and wholists, recapitulates an ancient quarrel between Democritus and Anaxagoras, a quarrel most obvious in psychology in the controversy between the behaviorists and the Gestalt psychologists in this century.

[2] I take description to be the primary task of all psychology. It is often counterposed to "explanation," with the notion that we first describe a phenomenon and later explain it. Explanation, therefore, is taken to be the final goal of science; it is the clarification of the necessary and sufficient conditions for the production of the event—roughly, what caused it. In my vocabulary, however, explanation is a special kind of description that describes events in terms of a cause-effect sequence. There are other descriptions that are perhaps more important, other formats of description that pull events into other kinds of focus. To say what something *means* to the man who asks the question is such a format. The result is not an outlining of necessary and sufficient conditions in a causal sense but an *interpretation*. All descriptions, including explanations, are interpretations anyway. An explanation offers us a certain interpretation; it says what something means within the framework of wanting to know what caused it, usually so that we can produce it or prevent it at will. It is possible, perhaps even desirable, to want to understand events for reasons other than to gain control over them. See Beshai (1971).

[3] The concept of *horizon*, initially spelled out by Edmund Husserl (1958), is a good deal broader than we are painting it here. In general, both Husserl and Martin Heidegger are in the Kantian tradition to the extent that, like Kant, they pursue their inquiries by asking what the preconditions are for something to be *possible*. This kind of question bears a superficial similarity to the seeking of causes or explanations as described in note 2. But the differences are monumental. To inquire into the possibility that *being is*, and that it is in such a way that certain beings can recognize it, is to describe the situation that we find ourselves in as human beings. It is a part of the ontological quest. To inquire into the necessary and sufficient conditions of a particular event is to ask a much smaller question, though not an unimportant one in practical terms. Rather than an ontological quest, Heidegger calls this latter inquiry an *ontic* enterprise. The relation between ontological and ontic enterprises is far from simple and will be discussed in Chapter 10.

At any rate, *horizonality* refers to the fact that human experience points beyond itself to a backdrop or ground that makes experience *possible*. Experience points to a network of already existing meanings that focus not so much on physical things as on their pattern or order, which we implicitly formulate in the act of being humanly conscious at all. There are lots of such patterns or orders (horizons) inherent in human experience; in the chapters in Part III we take up several such orders. As discussed in Part IV, the world is a very fundamental horizon.

[4] We have no intention of answering this question. Heidegger, in *Being and Time* (1962), says that *time* is the fundamental horizon of horizons, that there is no frame of meaning that outstrips time as the ultimate order of human experience, human being, and Being in general. Max Scheler (1954) and Martin Buber (1958) arrive at *an other* as the fundamental horizon. Maurice Merleau-Ponty (1962) describes the nature of human experience in such a way that *body* emerges as the fundamental horizon. Paul Ricoeur (1967, 1970) focuses on the symbol. Jean-Paul Sartre (1956) leans on the absolute otherness of things in themselves as they loom up unaffected by our consciousness. These descriptions are all, of course, oversimplifications—mere catchwords to indicate the directions in which our philosophical predecessors have gone. The important point here is that our psychology, an ontic enterprise, ultimately depends upon our ontological posture. However, to begin with a description of our ontological posture as a preliminary step to investigating experience would make this book into a very different kind of book—from my point of view an unreadable, if not unwritable, one. We must note that we (and all psychologists) are begging the ontological question and proceed nonetheless. The effect of this recognition should be to make us humble with respect to our conclusions. See also Chapter 10 for a discussion of ontological questions and their relation to psychology.

[5] The hyphenated phrase "being-in-my-office" is a somewhat awkward attempt to combine in one term the verbal term for the process of being and the nominal term for the locus of being. The experience described here is clearly both my *being* there and my being *there*. In the next paragraph, the same construction appears in the phrase "being-in-a-field," and later we shall become even more general and speak of "being-in-the-world." All these hyphenated expressions come directly from the German phenomenological literature, and they usually confuse if not offend American readers.

I have tried to use familiar American terms whenever possible and occasionally have used the terms "style," and "orientation to the world" when I thought they were just as good. However, there is no escaping the fact that new thoughts and new ways of thinking require new terms that sometimes make distinctions formerly unmade and sometimes combine things formerly distinguished. In all these "being-in" terms, we are combining being and locus, subject and object, consciousness and thing, because in experience they in fact occur together. Their separateness in our language is the result of our having hypostasized these two aspects of a prior unity, the result of the Western tradition that has made these abstractions into separable realities, violating the unity of experience as it is experienced and thus forcing us to use hyphenated phrases in order to describe experience accurately. See also Chapter 7, note 9.

[6] The verb "synthesizes" may be misleading in its implications that the fundamental units of experience are *the parts* and that the whole of experience is a mere makeshift or combination. Quite the opposite is true: The unity of experience is fundamental and original. Separation into parts is the result of a reflective analysis and always involves abstraction. The unity precedes the analysis, and the concrete precedes the abstract, both logically and empirically.

[7] In moving from "field" to "world" as we have, we have proceeded in a way that is convenient for our understanding, but it is quite different from the way in which the concept of "world" developed in the history of phenomenology. A brief recapitulation of that history may enhance our understanding of "world." Husserl (1958, 1960, 1968) spent his entire life investigating the nexus of interaction between the consciousness, which knows, and the object, which is known. His thought turned in the direction of a transcendental philosophy in which he postulated a transcendental ego, or absolute subject, not dissimilar to that of Kant. Such a turn seems to perpetuate the mind-body and mind-world dualisms, but Husserl's discoveries opened the way for subsequent phenomenologists to forgo the transcendental ego and these dualisms completely. One of these discoveries was that perception, the mere conscious reckoning of an object, always involves a horizon, or a background and context, within which the object becomes manifest. It is now obvious that such a horizon highly influences *what* we see when we apprehend an object. Husserl sought the fundamental horizon within which, or by virtue of which, there could be conscious experience at all. The various turns that his philosophy took in the early decades of this century were all attempts to clarify how it is that consciousness can come into some kind of contact with an object.

In the 1930s, after the Nazis retired him from his position at the University of Freiburg, which was then taken over by Heidegger, Husserl arrived at a formulation (1970) similar to Heidegger's formulation of "world" in the late 1920s: his concept of the *Lebenswelt*. Both he and Heidegger (1962), as well as later phenomenologists, discovered that it is the experience of "world" that is the horizon for any particular experience at all. Furthermore they found, first, that the horizon of the world is, in ordinary experience, implicit and difficult to articulate and, second, that the horizon of the world is not only essential to but fundamentally present within every perception. We never perceive an object in a vacuum but only through an orientation that marks out the dimensions of our "lived world," yet the intricacies of the lived world itself are so subtle as to be nearly invisible in our ordinary reckoning of our experience. For a good historical account of this entire situation, see H. Spiegelberg (1960).

Conceptually, we are tempted to inquire whether this "lived world" is the objective world, which is there whether we are or not, or the subjective world, which is totally relative to our personal apprehension. Such a choice seems forced on us by our traditional ways of thinking; this "world" must be *either* objective *or* subjective. Phenomenologists try to undercut the tradition that forces such a choice and to speak of "the world" as both objective and subjective—and as neither objective nor subjective.

The world, toward which behavior is directed and within which it must be understood, is not a *subjective* world. When I see you throw a dart at a target, it is not a *subjective* target you are aiming at; it is the target that is there for both of us, twelve feet away from you and twenty feet from me. But it is not merely an *objective* target either, for from my angle it invites throwing in a certain way with a certain arc and force, which is limited to my perspective and irrelevant to yours (see Chapter 10). But even further, your throwing of the dart emerges from your being-in-the-world, which has some differences from and some similarities to my being-in-the-world. If you are sexually frustrated, let us say, the behavior of throwing the dart may have a different force and flavor from those of my behavior if I am not. What you are bringing to the situation, however, is not a "motive" located somewhere inside you; rather, it is a world structure that gives the target, the dart, and the activity a certain meaning and coloration that is characteristic of your particular being-in-the-wolrd. If I am to understand the nuances of your dart throwing or your relation to a third person, I shall have to understand your world in its structure, your being-in-the-world. If I am to understand the behavior of a hungry rat in a maze, I must understand the rat's world; his hunger is not so much a "motive" driving him from within as much as it is a particular world structure or way of being-in-the-world. See L. Binswanger (1958a), E. Straus (1963), and Merleau-Ponty (1964c) for relevant discussions of animals.

This concept of "world" is similar to what K. Koffka (1935), a Gestalt psychologist, called the "behavioral environment," as opposed to the "geographical environment." The behavioral environment is the environment from the point of view of the behaving organism, and the geographical environment is the environment from the point of view of a neutral, outside observer. It is obviously the former that is most immediately important to understanding behavior. As Koffka put it, "only such movements of organisms are to be called behavior as occur in a behavioral environment" (p. 32). That is, movements that are not oriented to a perceived world, like being moved by the waves when swimming in the ocean or blown by the wind, are not *behavior* at all.

In general, positivists would argue that we can never know what the perceived world, or behavioral environment, is, for it is private and subjective. We must therefore build our science on the basis of the real world, the geographical environment, which is public and objective. We could indeed launch the opposite criticism to this distinction. We can never know what the real world, the geographical environment, is. The "neutral" perspective from which we reckon the geographical environment, the real

world, is not really neutral. It is part of our scientific or collective
perspective. Although it may be different from the phenomenological
"world" or the behavioral environment, the meaning of the distinction shifts
from one of "subjective" and "fantastic" versus "objective" and "real" to a
distinction between different perspectives. It is reduced, therefore, to the
distinction between private and public. We shall argue in Chapter 10 that
"subjective" worlds are profoundly shared and in Chapter 7 (note 3) that
privacy of experience has tended to be overemphasized in the Anglo-Ameri-
can philosophical traditions.

[8] The term "assumption" may be misleading if it is taken only in its
cognitive sense. Clearly, who-I-am-in-the-world is a matter of my being, not
only of my cognition. See also Chapter 8, note 2.

[9] One way to appreciate the pervasively integrating influence of world as
a context for our experience is to experience its disappearance. Some
reactions to drugs and psychotic crises may provide this experience (Keen,
1970, Chapter 12), and we can occasionally experience the weakening of its
integrating influence when contemplating the stars, cosmic space, cosmic
time, and so on.

[10] The metaphor of "enactment," like other operative terms used in the
text (staging, playing, role playing, construing), has a certain voluntaristic
flavor that points to, but surely does not resolve, profound philosophical
issues too complex to take up here. These dramaturgical metaphors were
introduced into psychology by Erving Goffman (1959) and extended by
Eric Berne (1964) and B. M. Braginski, D. D. Braginski, and K. Ring (1969).
They bring into focus the relative importance of compelling or sincere
motivation *versus* enactment of a role, script, part, myth, and so on. They
thus support the notion that human behavior is never simply or singly
motivated, a fact that makes phenomenological work that much more
urgent.

[11] Another formulation of this view of behavior in general would be to
characterize behavior as *referential*. Behavior *refers* to something beyond
itself. There are two senses in which this statement is true. First, from the
point of view of the behaving person, behavior is intentional and purposive;
we *mean* something by it—it is oriented toward something in our world.
Second, from the point of view of the interpreting observer of behavior,
behavior refers to that network of meanings and purposes that motivated it.
To John, his clenched fist *means* an impulse to strike. The behavior points
at some infuriating aspect of the world. To us, John's clenched fist *means*
he is angry. The behavior points to the anger. In the end, these two
references of the same behavior merge into one. When we interpret the
behavior as an expression of anger, we simultaneously interpret the anger as
a response to some aspect of the world that is infuriating him. This kind of
interpretation happens automatically in everyday life. As phenomenologists
we seek to make it explicit and rigorous. Naturally both stages of our

interpretation (that the clenched fist means anger and that the anger is because of such and such) are subject to error, but we are not powerless to check them out. The matter of erroneous interpretations will be taken up again in Chapter 3.

It is also well to point out that A. Schütz (1967) draws our attention to the ambiguity of calling an act an "expression." Some acts are intended to to communicate something to other people; others communicate without the actor intending them to do so; still others are not intended to communicate, and do not do so. These distinctions are important in a particular phenomenological analysis, but they do not affect our formulation here. Also see Chapter 9.

[12] The issue of unconscious motives and behavior is bound to come up in any psychology that takes conscious experience as its starting point. Certainly the events to which both Ivan Pavlov and Sigmund Freud direct our attention are important and must be recognized and taken into account. The Pavlovian event is most conveniently discussed in Chapter 7 and the Freudian event in Chapter 8. For now, let me add this much to what appears in the text. The "conditioned response," which clicks off without the intervention of consciousness, and the "unconscious wish," which motivates us in ways that we do not know may not be entirely different events, though the labels and the theories from which the labels are derived offer us very different interpretations indeed. There is the further difference in size: A conditioned response is a very small unit of analysis, a particular piece of behavior that is segregated from its context in life and studied in itself, whereas an unconscious wish engages us in a theory of one's total orientation to life throughout one's life history. But the similarity of the two views stands out from a phenomenological point of view. In each instance an action is performed in the context of some meaningful stimulus or situation. That the meaning is not apparent does not make the action or the stimulus situation meaningless. The task is to uncover the meaning. Pavlov and Freud attempted to do so in their theories of meaning, its origin and operation in our lives. Their theories are very different, but they have in common a concept of crucial machinery that operates *outside* conscious experience. It is as easy to see this crucial action *in* experience, but in order to do so we must view experience as horizonal, that is, as pointing beyond its explicit focus of attention to its backdrops or horizons, which are brought into explicit focus only by phenomenological work. These horizons are a part of experience in the sense that their presence is what makes experience what it is. That some of these horizons are not explicitly conscious is hardly a surprise if we view experience in its character as having multiple layers and multiple meanings. The fact that it is difficult to see some of the layers clearly is not surprising to anyone who has tried to do phenomenological work. On this entire problem, see also W. Fischer (1971), F. H. Lapointe (1971), and several papers in A. E. Kuenzli (1959).

In 1940 Wolfgang Köhler stated this entire issue in this way:

> Common human experience alone is not a material with which we can build a science of psychology. Indirect techniques reveal a great many functional relationships by which the contents and the course of mental events are determined. These facts of functional dependence often lie outside the range of direct awareness; and it seems important to realize that even the occurrence of experienced and understandable relationships in emotional life and in thinking is related to factors which are in the same sense but indirectly accessible. It is, I believe, no exaggeration if I say that every psychological investigation without exception will sooner or later reach a stage at which it must try to unearth such hidden functional relationships. (p. 42)

This objection by Köhler, whose work in Gestalt psychology is obviously an important contribution to phenomenological psychology, is surely one that is shared by many psychologists from Freudians to behaviorists. It is therefore very important to answer it. The objection rests on a distinction between "direct" methods (as in phenomenology) and "indirect" methods. The former are for inquiring into experience, the latter for inquiring into factors not given in experience—the germ that makes my head ache, the forgotten memory that makes me hate my boss, and so on.

As for the germ and other physical factors, including my physiological organism in general, something totally remote from my awareness shapes and conditions my experience and must be counted as one of the causal factors that lie behind it. Such functional relations are a part of psychology and are not amenable to phenomenological investigation. But their *relevance* to behavior is accessible to phenomenological investigation if they affect experience in any way. Except for the very few totally automatic kinds of behavior like reflexes, such functional relations always do affect experience.

The example of the forgotten memory is less clear, for the "forgotten" memory is not really forgotten. Its presence is not explicit; its presence shows itself only as a horizon of meaning in my experience of my boss. But to say that it cannot be explored directly is to limit direct exploration to focal consciousness and to rule out ahead of time an exploration of horizons.

[13] Neurosis and hypocrisy have something of this kind in common. Suppose that Mary is repelled by her husband's sexual advances, but instead of telling him so or trying to work out with him a way for him to be less repulsive she feigns fatigue, illness, and pain to release her from the obligation to express love sexually. Eventually she even *feels* tired and ill and suffers aches and pains when he begins his advances. Whether we call this behavior *neurotic* or *hypocritical* depends on whether we are in a diagnostic or judgmental mood.

At bottom, the two labels are very much the same; diagnostic language is often, if not always, an indirect and disguised vehicle for value judgments

(Keen, 1972; Szasz, 1970). In fact, diagnostic behavior is very similar to Mary's behavior when we look at them phenomenologically. Mary feels one thing, but, because the norms of marriage do not allow her to express them openly, she says something else and eventually comes to believe what she says instead of what she originally felt. Analogically, society feels repulsion and condemnation toward people who are sufficiently different, but, because the norms of our culture do not usually allow us to express these feelings openly (we are supposed to have sympathy for the mentally ill), we collectively say something else (or ask our doctors to do so) and eventually come to believe what we say instead of what we originally felt. In both instances, clarity between people is lost. Such a process is so common individually and socially that it must have been pointed out before. Indeed, that is the best interpretation of what Freud meant by "unconscious motives"—a concept, when seen in this light, not at all contradictory to a phenomenological analysis.

CHAPTER 3

[1] This point has not been particularly important in traditional American psychology, because so much of that psychology proceeds *as if* people were not people but objects that can be studied with the same methods that a physicist employs in broaching the physical world. The routines of physics have, in fact, almost become equated with science itself. Sigmund Freud's interpretive method and American "humanism" as practiced by Gordon Allport, Abraham Maslow, Carl Rogers, Rollo May, and others supply a continuing alternative view, indeed an alternative tradition in psychology. A. Giorgi (1970a) summarizes this tradition and also argues that changing our methods from those of physics to those of humanistic psychology, because of the nature of what we study, does not disqualify psychology from the category science. His vision of a *human science* is a late formulation of *Geisteswissenschaft* (in contrast to *Naturswissenschaft*) in German thought of the last century or so.

[2] This key methodological question is sufficiently different from traditional methodological concerns so that some comparison is perhaps in order. It is a mistake to polarize phenomenology and natural science too sharply, for they have many things in common, and polarization tends to lead practitioners of both to reject their important common ground. However, this methodological question may be compared to the traditional scientific one: How can we avoid subjective biases and arrive at objective truth? We can construe the situation as one in which the more open we as scientists are to phenomena in their uniqueness and in their various levels of meaning, the less certain of our conclusions we become. Conversely, the more certain of our conclusions we become, the more we have to focus on

specific, measurable meanings of the phenomena to the exclusion of all others.

The differing goals—appreciation of many-layered meaning and discovery of objective truth—have the common ground that we wish to *see clearly*. But whether it is more important to define clearly in terms of many-layered meaning or of objective truth—that is the question. Should we choose the objectively true, even if it violates the many-layered meaning or the many-layered meaning even if it violates the objective truth? To whom is the objective truth important? Does it matter if it is meaningful? To whom is many-layered meaning important? Does it matter if it is objectively true? For what purpose do we seek objective truth? For what purpose do we seek many-layered meaning? Which of these purposes is *our* purpose? These questions do not seem to allow a categorical decision between phenomenology and natural science, at least at this stage of our discussion.

[3] For a persuasive argument supporting this claim, see Wolfgang Köhler (1947) and F. From (1971). Köhler also offers (in his Chapter 7) an extremely interesting explanation of this phenomenon. He argues, according to the principles of Gestalt psychology, that there is a natural isomorphism between "dynamic developments in subjective experience" and "forms of perceived behavior" (p. 136). He also gives many similar examples in his study of apes (1925). Although his explanation ("isomorphism") is open to serious question, the fact that he took the phenomenon seriously enough to try to explain it is a substantial contribution to psychology.

[4] Martin Heidegger put it this way: "knowing is a kind of Being which belongs to Being-in-the-world" (1962, p. 88).

[5] Notice that this definition of *error* is not the usual one—inclusion of subjective bias—but rather is formulated as lack of clarity about that "bias." Because "there is no perspective-free knowledge" (a proposition most scientists agree with), how can we cleanse knowledge of perspective and bias? If that is impossible, then what becomes of the goal of objective truth? But the inclusion of a perspective in all knowledge does not rule out mutual *understanding*. Once people understand one another, they can also agree that each of them has part of the truth and that none of them has all of it. The inclusion of perspective rules out agreement only if someone claims that *his* perspective is better than that of someone else.

[6] The commonality of our world is not only the result of our sharing experiences. It is also the grounds or basis of our doing so. The common world is there first; our sharing is its fruit, rather than the other way around. This issue is taken up in Chapter 10.

[7] This line of thought and that taken up in note 5 tend to suggest that the pursuit of objective truth is hardly worthwhile if it costs us anything at all in terms of meaning. But there is indeed another side. Whereas all knowledge involves perspective, there is a perspective that can be not only *understood* by others but also *shared precisely* by others. That is, there is a way

of doing psychology in which I not only tell you about Ms. Smith from my point of view but I also describe that point of view—so that you can both *understand* it and *repeat* it. This approach requires cleansing my observations of everything personal, everything that is me, so that the information you receive from me is about Ms. Smith and not about how I personally see Ms. Smith; more accurately stated, it is about how I see Ms. Smith—in such a way that allows anyone to adopt my perspective and see precisely the same way. This strategy is that of psychological tests: the tester lets the test itself, which can be used by anyone trained to do so, do the essential perceiving. The tester himself merely reports the results. We do not therefore have perspective-free knowledge, for the test obviously *is* a perspective, but we also do not have merely personal, unverifiable, idiosyncratic knowledge. Perhaps this gain is worthwhile, even worthwhile enough to sacrifice some of the layers of meaning that are built into the phenomenological program. Perhaps we should be willing to know relatively little about Ms. Smith (for example, we may not know how angry she is chronically) if we can know it for sure; perhaps sacrificing the fuller understanding of her as being-in-the-world is worth it insofar as we gain a degree of certainty not available through an approach based on the hope that you will be able to see her clearly if only I do and if I describe my perspective to you fully enough.

Our view of this issue clearly depends on what the knowledge is *for*. If I want to prescribe psychiatric medicine for Ms. Smith, it is important to know whether or not to give her tranquillizing drugs. I am willing to sacrifice many nuances about what events mean to her and how she is-in-the-world, as long as I know what I need to know to prescribe the medication. On the other hand, if I am going to try to lead her to a better understanding of herself, then the index of anger that emerges from a psychological test is relatively meaningless to me without a context of how she is-in-the-world, even though I am relatively certain of that index and others like it.

Considered in this way, the questions in note 2 are reduced to whether we want to know Ms. Smith because we want to change her by some kind of curative treatment like drugs (the so-called medical model) or because we want to lead her into an understanding of herself. This complex issue has been dealt with elsewhere (Keen, 1972). See also Chapter 6, note 1.

[8] The phenomenological reduction was established as a methodological strategy by Edmund Husserl (1958, pp. 31–32, *passim*). A particularly lucid explanation is offered by R. M. Zaner (1970). Maurice Merleau-Ponty (1962) has commented, "The most important lesson which the reduction teaches us is the impossibility of a complete reduction" (p. xiv). Indeed, short of accepting Husserl's idealism, it would appear that Merleau-Ponty is correct. He goes on to comment:

> . . . radical reflection amounts to a consciousness of its own dependence on an unreflective life which is its initial situation, unchanging, given once and for all.

> Far from being, as has been thought, a procedure of idealistic philosophy, phenomenological reduction belongs to existential philosophy: Heidegger's "being-in-the-world" appears only against the background of the phenomenological reduction. (p. xiv)

Modern psychologists would surely concur that we cannot thoroughly cleanse ourselves of our preconceptions; thus we are thrown back to an examination of them as horizons of our own experience. In our account of the phenomenological reduction, we have not spelled this point out very fully, but we discover in performing the phenomenological reduction that the "inherent meaning" is not "out there" but is, rather, in the phenomena, which require our own being-in-the-world for their appearance at all.

For an excellent description of the process of examining our own horizons, a description that makes vivid the extraordinary rigor and effort involved in such a process, see A. Esterson (1972). Part I of Esterson's book is an analysis of a family with a schizophrenic daughter. This analysis makes clear the possibilities inherent in a phenomenological analysis and how it improves upon traditional psychiatric thinking. Part II is a description of his phenomenological method as "dialectical." This term refers to both the interpersonal nature of knowledge (emerging from dialogue) and also to a systematic tacking (to use Radnitzky's apt phrase, 1970) between immersion in a field of interpersonal action and detached, self-critical reflection, culminating in a creative new "totalization" of one's seeing of others. Esterson's description of his methodology and the fruits of his labors leaves little credence to the notion that phenomenology is either casual or produces casual results.

[9] This statement is another way of saying that all knowledge involves perspective. Of course, it is sometimes thought that the kind of science that aims at objective truth is somehow by-passing this problem. Because a phenomenological approach contains a number of assumptions, it too covers up as it reveals. Whereas the natural sciences, in seeking to root out error and to approximate truth as closely as possible, have developed elaborate techniques to increase certainty, phenomenology, in seeking to minimize the limits of perspective, has developed elaborate techniques to fill out our vision of the various layers of meaning.

[10] This statement is misleading if it is taken to imply that we all begin in a state of private consciousness and share bits and pieces only now and then. In Chapter 10 we shall make the point that the commonality of the world is *given, not achieved,* for human beings; it is always already there, even across radically different cultures. We know Ms. Smith and her perspective because we are all beings-in-the-world. Our prior commonality with her is just as impressive a datum as our differences. Our understanding of her uniqueness is always some variant of our prior understanding of ourselves and people in general as beings-in-the-world.

CHAPTER 4

[1] For a definitive account of this historical situation, see J. J. Kockelmans (1971) and especially H. Spiegelberg (1960, 1972).

[2] A quick survey of the phenomenological work that has been done in psychology can be achieved by looking at a relatively few sources. The *Journal of Phenomenological Psychology,* published at Duquesne University, is only a few years old. Other representative collections are those of A. Giorgi, W. Fischer, and R. Von Eckartsberg (1971), E. Straus (1964, 1966), M. Natanson (1973), and Spiegelberg (1972). An older collection is that of A. E. Kuenzli (1959). This listing does not take account of the philosophical literature (Merleau-Ponty's work, 1962, 1964b, 1964c, is highly psychological) or the voluminous European literature, translations of some of which are included in R. May, E. Angel, and H. Ellenberger (1958). J. Lyons (1961) offers a useful annotated bibliography of other sources scattered far and wide.

[3] Whether or not focusing on common features is *always* reductive is a difficult philosophical issue too entangled to discuss here. Edmund Husserl himself would likely quarrel with my way of putting it in the text.

[4] The implication of this line of thought is that we always interpret single, unique events before or in the process of comparing them and that we ought to interpret them as well as possible. In spite of this point, there may still seem to be a question about why we might want to understand an event in its uniqueness. Indeed, predictive science depends on events *not* being unique; its aim is to establish generalizations under which we can classify a unique event in order to understand it. Such understanding seems to suffice, even though the uniqueness of the event is lost.

Here again we are thrown back to the question of what the knowledge or understanding is *for,* which begs the question of our purposes—the nature of *our* style as scientists or psychologists in the first place. Such questions are personal and moral, prior to psychology, and not commonly understood to be within the province of psychology, *per se.*

It is worth pointing out, however, that, when psychology addresses itself to the lives of people, even to changing them, the moral issue is hardly avoidable—perhaps for the discipline as a discipline, as well as for its individual practitioners. The moral argument that psychology has an obligation to understand some events in their uniqueness, like the event of an individual mental patient, can be made on the basis of Western moral traditions to which we all probably subscribe (the integrity and dignity of the individual person, for example).

[5] This procedure is similar to what Giorgi (1966) has called "explicitation," which he describes:

> . . . if meaning [of the phenomenon] is to be understood it is done better by a process that for lack of a better term can be called explicitation, that is, the

process of making explicit or thematizing the locus of any given phenomenon within its horizon.

Whenever a phenomenon appears, it always appears within a certain horizon or context, and the horizon that implicitly is given with the phenomenon is not irrelevant for the understanding of the phenomenon. On the contrary the horizon is essential for the understanding of the phenomenon because the role that the phenomenon plays within the context, even if it is only implicitly recognized, is one of the determiners of the meaning of the phenomenon (Gerwitsch, 1964). (1971, pp. 41–42)

More specifically, we can reduce interview data to "intentional units," which are self-defining, self-delimiting aspects of the subject's experience. T. F. Cloonan (1971) used this method in investigating decision making.

⁶ We may ask of what value is such a finding? Why do psychologists spend time and effort arriving at such descriptions? Aside from the value that we can throw over it because of its similarity to art, such descriptions are critical for the theoretical assumptions of psychology, like that of the relation between body and mind. E. L. Stevick (1971) states:

As Schachter indicates, physiological arousal and a certain situation are essential components of emotion. However, this study reveals that both the subject's awareness of his situation and the role of bodily arousal are quite different than Schachter concluded. Because of his philosophical presuppositions, the body is for Schachter merely a physiological organism; he accepts the fact that it is aroused in emotion because he has experimental evidence to prove it. His studies use drugs to insure the presence of this arousal; he ignores or rules out that the arousal in emotion is self-initiated, and thus completely by-passes the crucial question–how does the body become aroused? Assuming a body/mind split, Schachter identifies awareness with reflection and thought. Therefore, he interprets his subjects' responding to the angry or euphoric situation as a cognition.

This study reveals, however, that emotion is a response of the whole person to a situation which is lived before it is reflected upon, and bodily arousal is part of of the way the subject lives the emotion; arousal is the body's affective mode. In anger, the arousal is one which thrusts the subject outward in explosive, expansive behavior. (p. 145)

See also Chapter 7, note 8.

This quote from Stevick is from *Duquesne Studies in Phenomenological Psychology: Volume I* by A. Girogi et al., and is reprinted by permission of Humanities Press, Inc., New York.

⁷ Almost certainly, the most important unanswered question that will occur to the critical reader is the question of *verification*. We have repeatedly made reference to the idea that adjudication of disagreements between interpreters must take place in the court of lived experience. But *whose* lived experience? If investigator A says X and investigator B says Y in interpreting an event and if they are both accurately describing their experience, then how are you and I to decide whether X or Y is the truth?

Are we reduced again to the prebehaviorist arguments, like that between W. Wundt and F. Brentano, with no way of making any progress?

This question begs a prior question: Why would we want to label X as "true" and Y as "false" in the first place? X is true to A, and Y is true to B. What is true to you and me? But this line of thought seems to take perspectivity so seriously that it is reduced to pure relativism; given such a radical relativism, it is hard to see why I would care to follow A's and B's work or why they would publish it.

This logical conclusion is true some of the time, but it is not descriptive of what usually happens. A and B probably do not differ absolutely. They probably overlap a good deal. My description of empathy as it appears in my experience is not *that* different from M. Lauffer's description. She sees it from one angle, I from another, you from yet another, but we all see the same thing. None of us is all worng. We can learn from one another how empathy, anger, or decision making looks from various perspectives and thus enrich our own. This concept of knowledge is different, to be sure,. from the notion of "objective truth" from which the question of verification arose in the first place. Perhaps it is a concept of knowledge that more closely suits our situation as psychologists than does the other one. Or perhaps it is preferable, in view of our answer to the question of what our knowledge is *for*. When we are reduced to that question, of course, we are thrown back to the people *we* are, as individuals and as psychologists, facing moral and ontological ambiguities.

Naturally, this line of thought leads to a rather different notion of what psychology as a discipline can be. J. Lyons (1970) spells some of this notion out (as do others) when he describes the relationship between a psychological researcher and his subject as a cooperative one, instead of the usual "looker—looked at" format. The data of psychology can become a "collection of informed perceptions which are appropriate to today's level of community understanding," instead of highly technical, unreadable, and esoteric findings of an elaborately instrumental pseudophysics. Lyons points out that "the most useful and enlightening collections of informed perceptions have been those of the talented literary figures of our culture." What has happened in the history of psychology has been that psychologists have tried to adapt the methods of physics to the study of people, making those changes that are necessary because of the changes in the subject matter but preserving the old concept of rigor. It is not clear why, except for historical accident, psychologists could not adapt the methods of literature to the study of people, making those changes that are necessary to achieve a degree of rigor but preserving the old concept of articulating the being-in-the-world of people. A less visionary and somewhat more concrete set of "next steps" for phenomenological-psychological research is suggested by Giorgi (1970b).

CHAPTER 5

[1] The issue of cultural imperialism is and has always been a problem in the social sciences. Our cultural history is permeated with examples of how in our very perception we are massively unconscious of its grounds, ranging from old notions of "the white man's burden" (see Van der Post, 1955, for a particularly sensitive account) through the evolutionary anthropologists (see Hofstadter, 1944) to contemporary mental-health practices (see Szasz, 1970). The most vivid examples of this kind of culturally imperialistic perception are to be found in the official justifications for war, most notably, the Vietnam war. Those who saw the American duty to save South Vietnam from North Vietnam were not wicked in any simple sense; they just did not know what or how they were seeing. Our imperialistic treatment of those minorities that have (or had) viable cultures (like the American Indians) is hardly an exception in the history of man. E. Pavenstedt's study is motivated by nobler sentiments, like her desire to eliminate the psychological suffering of poverty, but her perceptions are just as imperialistic. Her work too is hardly an exception in the history of the social sciences.

It is worth adding that phenomenology has no exclusive interest in avoiding cultural imperialism, and it has not the exclusive virtue of avoiding it. All science must try to avoid it, and I have heard of (but not seen) German phenomenological studies of Jews in the early 1930s that are primary sinners in this respect. It is perhaps unfortunate that these studies have not been translated so that we can discriminate good from bad phenomenology with their help.

[2] It is noteworthy that A. S. Niell (1960), responding to the tendency in our culture to be outrageously paternalistic to children, comes up with exactly the opposite conclusion. Now, the context is important here; Pavenstedt's families were hardly overprotective and paternalistic. But to insist that my needs as a father be indulged is hardly pathogenic. Everything hinges on what I communicate to my children in doing so. The real point is not the behavior *per se* but its meaning to the children. Demanding indulgence of my needs may communicate a sense of equality between us in some crucial respects, or it may communicate that I do not care about children at all. The critical issue is probably whether or not I care about them and can make that caring vivid in their experience.

[3] This failure is extraordinarily common in psychological studies of human beings. Many social-psychological experimenters attempt to manipulate the meanings that some experiences will have for the subjects by manipulating the formats of the experiments themselves. Giving instructions, telling a subject that the experiment is about X, boring him, frightening him, making him feel this way or that by giving him things to do or doing things

to him are all techniques of controlling the meanings of his behavior. The alternative strategy of *asking* him what his behavior means to him has been relatively rare because, first, it is difficult (without a theory of meaning and experience) to know what to do with such data and, second, the experimenter is often more interested in confirming a hypothesis that X conditions lead to Y behavior than he is in understanding the experience of his subjects or why, in their terms, they behave as they do. This issue will be taken up again later.

It is clear, however, that short-term meanings can be manipulated in an experimental way and that such manipulations occasionally imitate real life. For example, S. E. Asch's paradigm (1958), in which the subject makes a judgment in a context in which perceptual data tell him one thing and other people tell him something else, is not dissimilar to certain social situations in which conformity is produced. It differs, however, in that the subject never really forgets he is a subject in a psychological experiment, and the meaning of that fact alone, in terms of how he feels about himself, may influence his behavior mightily. Recent work on the social psychology of the experiment is beginning to come to grips with this problem (for example, Rosenthal, 1966; Orne, 1962). Alternatives to the experimental paradigm are not as well established as are the criticisms of them.

[4] One source of skepticism that we shall not discuss in the text deserves to be mentioned here, and that is the historically conditioned bias of behavioristic psychology that what a person says is not very important, even if it does indicate what he is experiencing, because experience is not an important part of the subject matter of psychology. Although we rarely see as bald a statement as that of John Watson (1924) anymore, psychologists are still prone to distrust, in principle, the slippery subject matter of consciousness and the verbal reports that express it. At the time when Watson wrote, the examination of consciousness was largely limited to the unfruitful routines of E. B. Titchener, and so Watson's categorical rejection of consciousness as subject matter came as a breath of fresh air. I hardly need to say that it seems to me that the baby was thrown out with the bath, however, and that psychologists evolved into the peculiar posture, still common today, of trusting verbal reports from their spouses, children, and friends—in fact relying heavily on them in virtually every facet of everyday life—but distrusting them immensely in the laboratory. This peculiarity has contributed to whatever irrelevance modern psychology has to everyday life.

[5] The experimental manipulation of meaning, as in the Asch (1958) experiment, may well be construed as a way of asking and listening. It is, of course, an indirect way. Asch does not ask his subjects whether or not they conform and why; rather, he puts them into a situation in which they do conform and then tries to figure out why by manipulating certain variables like the instructions, the size of the group, the unanimity of the stooges, and so on. (Asch did interrogate his subjects after the fact, but that

procedure never contributed a systematic part of the data.) Asch "asks" about conformity, then "listens" to the answer in the subject's behavior. Such experimental routines do not overcome the problems of the roles of examiner and examined. A subject never forgets that he is a subject and behaving in that role, which influences his behavior.

[6] Lyons (1970, 1963) has described this strategy in detail. It has been called to my attention by a friendly critic that the method that I apparently have in mind has already been invented and widely developed and used by cultural anthropologists, at least since the time of Bronislaw Malinowski. I immediately recognize that this comment is strikingly true in one sense. "Participant observation," a data-gathering technique that requires the observer to participate in the social reality that he is observing in order to observe it properly, has a great deal to offer to psychology. In an eleventh-hour attempt to find helpful references for the reader along these lines, I have found too much material to recommend. However, L. J. Goldstein's article (1947) is quite to the point. Leon Festinger's study (Festinger, Riecken, and Schachter, 1956) offers a similar example from social psychology, as does that of William F. Whyte (1943).

The controversy about participant observation applies to phenomenological method in a very peculiar way. On the one hand, Malinowski argued that research on human behavior must "grasp the native's point of view, his relation to life, to realize *his* vision of *his* world" (quoted in Kardiner and Preble, 1961), yet an anthropological field worker in a foreign culture cannot entirely cease bearing *his* own native culture. Furthermore, he must have some categories of analysis in mind that are *not* native to the culture he is studying, if he is to produce a study *about* that culture, rather than one that merely expresses that culture.

On the other hand, whereas total "participation" is neither possible nor desirable in anthropology, *some* participation, even if vicarious, is surely necessary in order to understand at all fully what one is observing.

This dilemma, quite vivid for anthropological methodologists whose target is culture, appears even more forcibly for a phenomenologist, whose target is human being. There is no way to "get out of the human situation" in order to study it, no way to achieve the perspective of God. Thus Maurice Merleau-Ponty (1962) says that "the most important lesson which the [phenomenological] reduction teaches us is the impossibility of a complete reduction." Yet it does not follow that we have no possibility of improving upon the "natural attitude." All human investigation of human being is perforce "participant observation," and so the development of that technique by anthropologists holds an inevitable fascination for the human investigator of human being.

With respect to gathering data from informants as participant observers do, I recommend Jules Henry's study (1971) as a model. The work of Malinowski (1948) and Margaret Mead (1935) is certainly suggestive from a methodological point of view.

[7]It is perhaps important to distinguish the "subject as coresearcher" idea from the prebehaviorist introspectionist research strategy of W. Wundt and E. B. Titchener. Introspection, as a technique, requires extensive training and, when such training is available, elaborate ideas about what is to be found. Disagreements were at one time adjudicated by having the "most expert" introspectionist decide what the true shape of the mind was. Phenomenological techniques may come to the same fate at times. But, in contrast to Titchener's experiments, everyday understanding, which is the basis of all research, is the focus of the phenomenologists; it is not held in contempt as it was by the introspectionists. This fact makes an important difference in that argument. At any rate, the introspectionist was also a coresearcher, and the sense of a task in common with the experimenter was an important part of that routine as well. The difference, however, is that the present strategy does not depend on rigorous training of the subject. As a matter of fact, it is exactly everyday experience, in its untrained and natural state, that we seek to explore and describe.

[8]This problem was solved by Freud through the technique of free association in a lengthy and laborious routine, no doubt an impressive procedure. Since Freud, a number of other strategies have emerged that are less time consuming but still approach our goal. Carl Rogers (1942), working in a relationship specially designed to help people (see Chapter 6), repeated the client's thoughts in somewhat different words, allowing the client to correct every communication at every step of the way. S. Jourard (1964, 1971) has systematically explored the conditions and techniques of self-disclosure and makes many valuable suggestions about overcoming this difficulty. F. Deutsch and W. F. Murphy (1955), writing of a more directive interview technique within the psychoanalytic tradition, argue that two questions— "What do you mean?" and "How do you know?"—enable an interviewer to evoke the necessary experiential report without telling people what to say. The original methodologist along these lines was no doubt Socrates.

This method of asking the subject what we want to know was not used in the episode described in Chapter 1 and to visualize using it there brings a number of problems with the method into focus.

[9]R. M. Zaner (1970) offers a particularly cogent argument that such suspension is possible. He points out that it was Edmund Husserl's ideal all along. Merleau-Ponty, in his essay "Phenomenology and the sciences of man" (in Merleau-Ponty, 1964b), offers an equally lucid demonstration that the critical advances in science have always followed this pattern instead of the theory of induction inherited from John Stuart Mill.

[10]It is generally less outrageous to assume that people will understand us when we try not to deceive them than to assume that they will not understand when we try to deceive them. The latter assumption is built into experiments in which the purposes are concealed; the former assumption is built into an honest conversation as we are describing here. It is also

easier to assume people will be honest when they trust us than it is to assume
that their behavior is revealing of how they are when they do not—such as
when we try to deceive them, and to deceive them into thinking we are not
trying to deceive them.

[11] One colleague referred to this study as "journalistic"—indicating his
disparagement of Henry's lack of more traditional scientific methodology.
The remark is interesting. Journalists enjoy a long tradition of reporting to
us what we cannot see and they continue to have considerable social power.
At the same time, that group contains perhaps some of the best and worst
scientists (in the broad sense of investigating and reporting). Of the best, we
would probably say their work is similar to Henry's in their scrupulous
attention to what they experience, their critical-reflective attitude, and their
communication of carefully written portraits. The worst of the journalists
may be truly frightening as propagandists, but traditional science is not the
only correction for such shortcomings. Being a good journalist is another
correction, and like Henry's work, this requires an attitude approaching the
phenomenological. See Chapter 4, note 7, and Lyons (1970) when he
speaks of the proper output of psychology as a "collection of informed
perceptions which are appropriate to today's level of community
understanding."

CHAPTER 6

[1] This view of clinical psychology is somewhat controversial. For a discussion of the relations among traditional psychology, the so-called medical
model, and phenomenological psychology, see Keen (1972).

In general, we may say, picking up from Chapter 3, note 7, that the
medical model is incompatible with a phenomenological approach to clinical
psychology. The medical model implies, first, a role relationship in which
"doctor" and "patient" are roles assigned permanently, fixing and contain-
ing the meanings that experience in the clinical situation can have; second,
that perception of "the problem" as something gone wrong in the internal
workings of the patient (or in his "mind"); third, operation upon the
patient in the fashion in which a doctor "fixes" one's body—without the
necessity of the patient's understanding the intricacies of the treatment.
Not all psychotherapists who work in their offices operate according to all
aspects of the medical model; in fact, they violate it freely. But it is the
center of gravity of the psychiatric tradition and is vividly represented in a
number of such common practices as administration of drugs, electroshock,
psychosurgery, and some versions of behavior modification. It is interesting
that practitioners of behavior modification claim to have overcome the
medical model (Bandura, 1969). They have done so in some respects, but in

others behavior modification is an exaggeration of the psychiatric tradition
—for example, in the role definitions.

[2] It may be important to note that not all phenomenologists would agree
that the center of meaning resides in each one of us. Jean-Paul Sartre may
be able to accept such a way of putting it; Martin Heidegger, especially in
his later work, would reject it outright.

[3] Operating in life in the service of a self-concept is certainly inevitable,
but in becoming rigidified we approach the postures of Ms. Downs or Mr.
Pinky (discussed in Chapter 8). Rogers is not the only theorist to have
noted this aspect of personal problems. See also Karen Horney (1950) and
Keen (1970), for example.

[4] The list could be practically endless, and so we shall limit ourselves to
some of the psychologists who are most obviously in the phenomenological
tradition, who explicitly take up psychotherapy, and whose work is available in English. V. E. Von Gebsattel, R. Kuhn, and H. Ellenburger all have
relevant essays in R. May, E. Angle, and Ellenburger (1958). M. Boss (1958,
1963) most obviously takes a Heideggerian approach to psychotherapy.
Few of F. J. J. Buytendijk's essays are available in English, but his study of
pain (1962) is a highly relevant phenomenological essay. Binswanger (1963)
and Van den Berg (1973) have excellent cases in English. J. F. T. Bugental
(1965), May (1967), A. Burton (1967), and Keen (1970) are all Americans
who have taken a phenomenological approach to psychotherapy. R. D.
Laing (1967, 1969) offers many relevant insights. Other articles on therapy
may be found in the *Journal of Phenomenological Psychology*, the *Review
of Existential Psychology and Psychiatry*, and the *Journal of Existential
Psychiatry*.

[5] Naturally, the tester and the client do not always have to agree, and the
tester's perceptions are part of the report too. If the tester says that the
client worries a lot about his adequacy as a male, for example, and the client
does not see it that way, but rather sees his worries as financial, occupational,
and so on, then, first, the client's perception and interpretation of his own
worries are at least as important as those of the tester, and, second, we would
wonder about the kind of data that could lead the tester to his conclusion in
the face of the client's disagreement. What he, the tester, means by such an
interpretation must certainly be clarified, and the tester, the client, and the
reader of the report all stand to benefit from such clarification. It is worth
noting that "the court of lived experience" as it is brought to bear in this
situation does not lead us into the problems of verification discussed in
Chapter 4, note 7, for it can be taken for granted that people have different
perspectives and that each is a valid and valuable one to learn about. This
situation, with all its advantages, could predominate in all psychology
dealing with human beings if we were interested in making it predominate.
Clinical psychologists may argue that something would be lost. It is worth
inquiring just *what* that would be.

[6] Of course some of the goals of clinical psychology as it is now defined would not be met in this way. The manipulation of behavior would be much less simple, perhaps impossible, through this approach. Whether or not this goal seems critical depends upon *values* (whether or not we should manipulate people for their own good, regardless of whether or not they understand) and *approaches* (the medical model or some other one). Also the science of objective truth about the nature of the psyche would not flourish (if it ever has), and we would have to replace it with the "collection of informed perceptions appropriate to the level of community understanding" currently given us by literary and journalistic experts in our culture. Whether or not we can settle for that, instead of for the expert-oriented knowledge of a technical science, also depends on our values and approaches (see Chapter 11).

CHAPTER 7

[1] The concept of *field* has a long and distinguished history in psychology. The field theorist *par excellence* was Kurt Lewin (1935, 1936), whose concept of field is a combination of the biologist J. von Uexküll's concept of *Umwelt*, or the environment as perceived by an organism; field theory in physics, as in electromagnetic theory developed in the nineteenth and twentieth centuries; and astute psychological observation, which convinced him that the point of view of the behaving actor is crucial in understanding action. Figure 5 in Chapter 1 is typical of Lewin's kind of thinking, though he often became more abstract. He sought to use a small number of concepts, like vector, valence, barrier, channel, and positive and negative poles, to describe all situations within which behavior takes place. This theoretical strategy has the advantage of great generality and the disadvantage of losing the uniqueness of a situation, which the concept of physiognomy permits. Many American psychologists have been highly influenced by Lewin, especially in the study of small groups. Edward Tolman (1966), unlike most Lewinians, was simultaneously a behaviorist whose experimental work was largely with rats. Tolman's concept of a "cognitive map" points to the rat's experiential field, and it gained legitimacy within behaviorism by means of Tolman's billing it "an intervening variable," necessary to explain the observed relation between stimulus and response—the measurable anchors of all behaviorist theory. Although Tolman was also not interested in a field's physiognomy, like Lewin and like the phenomenologists, and unlike other behaviorists, he was convinced that the point of view of the actor is important in understanding behavior.

[2] This statement is not literally true, but our native ability to see from another's point of view is one of the basic facts of human psychology that has not been sufficiently appreciated, perhaps because of the empiricist

tradition in Western thought, which says that we "know" only what we receive through our sense organs. I obviously understand the experience of others all the time without this understanding having emerged from a discrete sensory channel. This issue has been discussed in relation to methodology in Chapter 3.

[3] The difference between the two ways in which we structure our own fields by our own initiative is not as great as it seems. When seeing situations in a certain way, we are presumably operating in a purely private, subjective sphere, and, when behaving overtly to affect them, we are presumably operating in a purely public, objective sphere. But both spheres are far from pure. Our presumably *private experience* is usually "written all over our faces"—and all over our postures and gestures. We can have secrets, but keeping them is very difficult. Our presumably *public behavior* refers directly to our experience (Chapter 2, note 11) in the mind of any beholder. When I enter a situation cautiously, brazenly, fearfully, or whatever, I structure it as a whole, not first as a visual spectacle and then as a behavioral field. My perceptual presence and my behavioral presence in the situation are of a piece, integrated with each other so thoroughly that the analytic distinction between perception and behavior seems questionable.

All in all, the distinctions between public and private, objective and subjective, behavior and experience are drawn all too rigidly in traditional American psychology. The fact that we have traditionally made this distinction so strictly betrays our indebtedness to the implicit ontology embedded in much of Western thought, which Martin Heidegger clearly tried to overcome. Western privatistic and subjectivistic ontology makes it difficult to see how we understand one another in everyday life as we in fact do. By inquiring into the grounds of possibility of everyday experience, by looking for the horizons of experience within which experience comes to have the meaning it does, we discover a distinctly social level of meanings; see Chapters 9 and 10.

If consciousness were primarily private, made public only occasionally when we explicitly expose it to one another, then our experience of other people would be more like looking at a pile of phonograph records than like the rapport, empathy, and understanding that characterize everyday life. Furthermore, consciousness is *public* not only in the sense that it is difficult to keep secrets; it is public also in the sense that members of the same culture always share expectations, norms and role concepts. These shared aspects of our consciousness are not merely *added in* to otherwise private consciousness; they supply the framework of meanings within which we locate our own privacy.

Therefore behavior is *more explicitly* public and objective than the way in which we subjectively see situations, but it is a relative distinction. Public and private are two poles of a continuum; most of the critical action is somewhere between them. Furthermore, this continuum is less a matter of metaphysical realities than of the degree of explicitness and the degree to which we are held socially accountable.

[4] For a fuller phenomenological study of the Müller-Lyer illusion, see R. J. Alapack (1971). Alapack asked a number of subjects to describe the figures, without directing their attention to the issue of length, and was able to demonstrate that our relation to these figures is more complex than the usual "illusion" that they create. Particularly, Alapack's method was similar to those described in Chapter 4 (see especially note 5), and he concluded that our bodily orientation is an apsect of our experience, verifying Maurice Merleau-Ponty's (1962) conclusions.

[5] There is a significant complication at this point. Does the car become physiognomically larger as it approaches? Perhaps we could argue that the physiognomy of traffic is so strongly influenced by our knowledge that the car is the same size that the car does *not* appear larger as it approaches. Perhaps we are tempted to say that it grows larger physiognomically only because we *know* that its image on our retina grows larger. There is no absolute answer to this question, no absolute physiognomy that is naïve to what we know about spatial relations in the world. Next time you walk down a hallway, watch the walls, ceiling, and floor flow past you; it can become spooky. Is this experience "more natural" or "more fundamental" than our ordinary experience of moving from place A to place B? It is well to become sensitive to physiognomies like the spooky hallway, but our term "physiognomy" ought to refer equally to both experiences. A "pathway" from A to B is not purely conceptual and nonphysiognomic; it merely has a different physiognomy.

[6] This statement is actually very controversial philosophically, for it is possible to argue that numbers constitute a perfectly coherent meaning context without reference to anything that we experience in the world. Our view here is more "existential"; that is, we hold that our concrete existence in the world is inevitably the ground of all meaning.

[7] It may be helpful to clarify the relation between the distinctions abstract versus concrete and public versus private. They have overlapping but far from identical meanings; we may see how they cut across each other in the following chart.

	public	private
abstract	1	3
concrete	2	4

Cell 1 contains those shared meanings that are embedded in language. It is clear that abstractions from experience (as in language) are easier to share than immediate experience, which is an intransigently private anchor in the unique experience of the unique individual. Cell 2 is not empty, however; we share the Müller-Lyer illusion, the experience of the empty theater, and many other very concrete physiognomic experiences. This sharing indicates that, although experience has an anchor in the uniqueness of the individual, it is hardly exclusive, even in its concreteness. Cell 3 is also not an empty cell, though abstractions are usually social. Cell 4 is for the intransigently private and concrete: mysical experiences that are indescribable, for example.

[8] The theorist who best describes our behavioral orientation in space is Merleau-Ponty. Such a purposive orientation in space is often bodily, and Merleau-Ponty is also the theorist of choice with respect to the phenomenology of the body. In his major theoretical work, *The Phenomenology of Perception* (1962), he elaborates the understanding of Schneider, mentioned earlier in this chapter. His summary comment on the point we are trying to make about our relation to "field" and how body is implicated:

> If bodily space and external space form a practical system, the first being the background against which the object as the goal of our action may stand out . . . it is clearly in action that the spatiality of our body is brought into being, and an analysis of one's own movement should enable us to arrive at a better understanding of it. By considering the body in movement, we can see better how it inhabits space (and, moreover, time) because movement is not limited to submitting passively to space and time, it actively assumes them, it takes them up in their basic significance. . . . (p. 102)

Our bodily orientation in space is so fundamental that we are likely to overlook it, especially when we think about human beings, most of whom construe life largely through ideas instead of physical relations. However, a close look at experience reveals that this kind of horizon is always present and essential to the meaning of events. Often it is quite crucial, as when certain kinds of situations make us emotional. Emotion is a bodily response, as well as an ideational one. It is, of course, synthesized in concrete experience and appears as physiognomic field properties.

Perhaps the most elaborate descriptions of emotional experience in its bodily aspect are given by Jean-Paul Sartre (1956). For another example of the integration of bodily meanings in experience, see the study of anger by E. L. Stevick (1971) reported in Chapter 4. Stevick's study also makes it clear how a phenomenological approach to emotion obviates the classical "mind-body problem":

> Traditional studies of emotion deal with the body as an object in the world while ignoring it as lived by the consciousness. They observe and measure the changes which this object undergoes in emotion while never solving the problem of how or why these changes occur, and the how and why is an important question for their consideration precisely because the body is for them a physiological organism separate from the "mind." But the data of this experiment show subjects describing their bodies as that which lived and through which they lived their anger. With this presupposition, the body's being permeated through and through with anger so that it spontaneously bursts forth

to preserve its *ability* which is its very being in the world is no longer a problem or even a question for the psychologist. (p. 147)

W. Fischer (1970) has also integrated bodily and other meanings in the experience of anxiety. The mind-body problem is perhaps the best and most troublesome example in Western thought of making an analytic distinction, verifying the distinguished elements, then finding it impossible to describe the *relations* between the analytically separated parts. As in our distinction between "abstract" and "concrete" experience in this chapter, the solution to the problem of "relations" is to return to the lived experience from which the parts were abstracted, where we find no "relation among separate parts" at all but an integrated whole whose organization is its own and not beholden to our conceptual abstractions.

[9] As we have made a point of the notion of being *in* space, it is well to note that Martin Heidegger (1962) has decisively pointed out how much meaning is carried by the word "in." Being-in-the-world is a hyphenated term indicating an experiential unity from which "man" and "world" are abstractions. Therefore the "in" is not the same as when we say the cigar is *in* the box. "There is no such thing as 'side-by-sideness' of an entity called 'Dasein' with another entity called 'world.'" (p. 81). Objects are side by side, and that is the sense in which the cigar is *in* the box—the sense of physical proximity. To say we are "in" the world or "in" the field is to describe a very different sort of relationship or, again as before, the notion of "relationship" suffers from the assumption that the analytically separated parts (man and world) are *separate* and must be *related* conceptually. Hence the "in" is neither merely physical (cigar in the box) nor does it reflect a relationship between man and world. Heidegger's "in," and ours, is an expression of the experiential presence of the world to man, a presence such that each is a horizon of the other and neither makes sense apart from the other. I am-in-the-world in the sense that I am *open to* the world (which is not how the cigar is *in* the box), but being open is not a characterization of myself and my relation to something "out there"; this openness or "clearing" is prerequisite for there to be experience at all. In this line of thought we can see, first, the return to experience as it is experienced, instead of as it has been conceptualized between man and world, and second, a seeking of the prerequisites that must be articulated instead of a building of abstractions into theory. Both ways of thinking characterize phenomenological philosophy and are distinct from more traditional ways of thinking; see Chapter 2, note 5.

CHAPTER 8

[1] From a Heideggerian point of view, this statement is a very weak one. More accurately, we say that *Dasein* (Heidegger's term for human presence,

more typically referred to by the misleadingly abstract term "man"—see Chapter 7, note 9) *is* a temporalizing, a making time, a timing. Time is not something "out there" that we are "in"; it is an activity of *Dasein*—indeed the most fundamental activity of *Dasein* and hence the most fundamental horizon of human experience. Not that time is a voluntary choice. We have no choice *whether or not* to make time; it is inevitable that we do so. Time, like the world, is integrated into that experiential unity that is our first datum and, like the world, has been abstracted for special consideration in Western thought. Because of this tradition, which has created the "problem" of the "relation" between time and self, we must now work our way back to the unity of experience in order to start anew. This chapter is aimed at reintegrating self and time, but we do not want to keep it a secret that they are already of a piece in experience and that, if we can open ourselves to experience as experienced, conceptual work as in this and succeeding paragraphs is unnecessary.

[2] This phrase, "the assumption that he has a future," may be misleading if "assumption" is taken in its purely cognitive sense. The more proper phenomenological way to put this notion would recognize that the future penetrates the present (rather than being an assumption or premise of it). The present is not separate from the future but is even now a *presencing of* or *making present of* the future. The less awkward, but also less phenomenologically accurate, wording in the text was selected for purposes of simplicity.

[3] This line of thought may be deceiving in that "is" and "are" have been reduced in this syllogism to an equal sign, denoting sheer equality. Logically, this procedure is sound enough. But phenomenologically, to say "We *are* our histories and futures" is to say more than that "we" and "our histories and futures" are identical. The sentence really also states that we *live* our histories and futures; we appropriate them and enact them. The verb "are" indicates something quite beyond mere logical equivalence; it indicates *being*, as in being-in-the-world. Like the word "in," in the last chapter, simple words must bear a lot of meaning when they are used to describe experience as it is experienced, instead of to indicate mere logical conjunctions. This difficulty is inherent in reading phenomenological literature, and it is overcome only by reading phenomenologically.

[4] This conceptualization of guilt may seem at first very different from more standard ones like that of Sigmund Freud. According to Freud, guilt may pervade my life because of a long-forgotten episode or situation for which I felt as a child, in the childish reckoning of things, guilty. Masturbation and parental disapproval, or Oedipal wishes to possess mother exclusively, with fantasied paternal retaliation, exemplify such a situation (see Freud, 1961). According to our present formulation, I would seem to have to *remember* such events consciously in order to feel guilty. Nearly a century of psychoanalytic experience disproves such a claim. In fact, the

term "having forgotten" or "having repressed" the memory is really only a way of saying that many horizons of our contemporaneous experience are difficult to focus on and articulate. When we do "remember," as in psycho-analytic insight, we do not so much make conscious something that was "unconscious" as we achieve an articulation of a horizon of contemporary experience and an explicit grasp of one of the premises of all our life experiences. The process is not one of digging up a fact from the past but one of bringing to light the meanings of our contemporary experiences and allowing them to be reinterpreted. Phenomenologists are not the only ones to have understood psychoanalysis in this way; see also H. Fingarette (1963). The most thorough phenomenological interpretation of Freud's work is that of P. Ricoeur (1970).

Other phenomenological literature on guilt may be found in Martin Buber (1957), G. Haigh (1961), and Ernest Keen (1966). It may also be useful to note that the notion of guilt in the text also has a particular relation to Heidegger's notion (1962) of "being-guilty." He would call our description an "existentiell exemplification" of the more primordial "exis-tential" state of being-guilty. The relation of "existentiell" to "existential" is the same as the relation of "ontic" to "ontological," as discussed in Chapter 10.

⁵ See Antoine's "romance" of "perfect moments" in Jean-Paul Sartre's *Nausea* (1959).

⁶ It is perhaps important to point out that this notion of health is much more Sartrean than Heideggerian. Indeed, Heidegger speaks of an ontologi-cally given "repetition," which is an essential limit on the future.

⁷ The term "extravagance" was first used by Ludwig Binswanger (1963) to refer to that kind of self-definition that has no respect for what is *given*. The interaction between what is given and *necessary*, on the one hand, and what is open and *possible*, on the other hand, is one of the oldest and knottiest problems in the history of philosophy. Neither extreme view is adequate; total freedom is as far from man's condition as is total determinism. There is the danger here, once again, of making an abstracted part of lived experi-ence (making a choice or being compelled by factors beyond our control) paradigmatic for the human condition. Having seen that freedom and determinism are both characteristic of human experience and having solidi-fied and made absolute both interpretations, we now find ourselves stuck with the "problem" of the "relation" between the two. There is no "solu-tion" to this problem on a conceptual level. The phenomenological response here, as always, is to return to lived experience, where we find the two aspects of human experience already integrated and horizonal for each other. Each comes into focus as an experience only against the backdrop of the other. We notice our freedom because it stands out from our limitations, and we notice our determinateness because it stands out from our freedom. However, we may add that even this description, which is true as far as it

goes, still polarizes freedom and determinism, as if they were separate aspects of experience. In my everyday life, I proceed about my business in light of a being-in-the-world that is both free and determined simultaneously. I do not undergo a cognitive categorization of each aspect of experience and calculate the extent of my freedom before I perform each action. I already *know* how the possibilities and necessities stack up, and I proceed accordingly. The fact that this *knowing* is subject to change, as in psychotherapy, which may liberate Ms. Downs and Mr. Pinky, merely indicates that being-in-the-world is in a constant state of flux. A therapist may see the *possibilities* of changing (against the *necessities* of being bound to be who one is) somewhat differently from the way Ms. Downs or Mr. Pinky see them. They will not be persuaded by his arguments, but they may come to acquire a view closer to his if they come to see clearly the horizons of their experience and how the meanings of events have built up like sediment over the years. Such a change, however, is not merely intellecutal; it is a change in the very structure of their experience and hence in the character of their being-in-the-world.

CHAPTER 9

[1] See Chapter 2, note 13.

[2] Many interpersonal agreements are specifications of already existing agreements that are present in society even before we engage in them: the phenomenon of *roles*. There was a *father role* before I was a father, a *husband role* before I was a husband, a *student role* before I was a student, a *middle-class, Midwestern child role* before I was a middle-class, Midwestern child, and so on. Even though the phenomena of roles have traditionally been the province of sociology and social psychology, we must recognize that the structure of roles and expectations that make up our social organization (or culture) inevitably supplies a horizon for most interpersonal agreement that does not take place within this context. Indeed, there is a phenomenological social psychology (Von Eckartsberg, 1971; Schütz, 1967, 1970; Kwant, 1965), which has been left out of this book but which we dare not ignore if we are to have a phenomenological study of some behavior that is loyal to the meanings as they in fact appear in our experience. Erving Goffman's "microsociology" is very useful for phenomenological work (1959, 1961, 1971). See also the provocative book by M. Natanson (1970).

We may say, generally, that our focus on meanings and horizons would not change in a phenomenological sociology. Many meanings are *shared*; they are the property of a group primarily and of individuals only to the extent that they are members of the group. Indeed, sharing the meanings of the collective is a measure of membership, and group members who know implicitly (sometimes explicitly) who is "in" or "out" of a group are responding to the degree to which the individual shares the collective meanings. Not only are meanings shared, however; they are also *historical*. To say "A Rockefeller would not do that'" is to make reference to a *tradition*. Tradition is a shared history within which the experience of the individual takes place, ensuring it of common or collective meanings. Tradition is always already present; it is a horizon of experience in individuals, and that is how we can come to know it if we want to study it and make it explicit. Part of what we know implicitly when we are members of a tradition is that others in the tradition share these meanings with us. A phenomenological sociology can make all this material clear.

[3] *Confirmation* appears in the work of R. D. Laing (1969), but he took it from Martin Buber (1958). *Collusion* is also taken from Laing (1969). The term *pretension* has not been used before in this way, as far as I know. The entire idea is not dissimilar to Eric Berne's notion of *game*, made famous a few years back by his best seller, *Games People Play* (1964), and perpetuated on the best-seller list by T. A. Harris, *I'm Okay — You're Okay* (1967) and M. James and D. Jongeward, *Born to Win* (1971). The popularity of this kind of psychology with the general public is beginning to rival the popularity of Sigmund Freud half a century ago, though the mystique of Freud in the 1920s (Anderson, 1967) and his enduring impact upon our culture (Rieff, 1959) may never be matched again. For an analysis of this situation, see Ernest Keen (1972).

[4] The study of families has flourished in the past decade in the professions of psychiatry and psychotherapy. Some examples of the current literature are V. W. Eisenstein (1956); I. Boszormenyi-Nagy and J. L. Framo (1965); T. Lidz, S. Fleck, and A. Cornelison (1965); J. G. Howells (1971); G. H. Zuk (1971); A. Ferber, M. Mendelsohn, and A. Napier (1972); Laing and A. Esterson (1970); Esterson (1972), and the volume by the Group for the Advancement of Psychiatry, *Treatment of Families in Conflict* (1970).

[5] See Laing (1967) for an understanding of the family as "a mutual-protection racket."

[6] See Laing and Esterson (1970) for examples of this "vindictiveness." Their subjects, like most families, do not consciously attempt to hurt the family deviants. Indeed, often the opposite is true of their explicit representations of their own motives to themselves. This vindictiveness is "unconscious," by which we mean that the behavior responds to a situation the meaning of which comes from horizons of which we are not focally aware. Of course, these horizons are nevertheless built into our experience on an implicit level.

[7] See Chapter 9, note 2.

[8] See Chapter 2, note 6.

[9] A concluding complication for this entire chapter: Interpersonal relations are seen here largely as a matter of "making deals." This view implies that a fundamental human motivation is to preserve one's own

identity. If this is true, it would call into question the already given commonality of the *world*, for which we shall argue in the next chapter. If the view implicit in this chapter is carried through to its conclusion, the commonality of the world would not be already given but would be a universal collusion, a universal deal, a common consent to play the same game. The fact that there are individuals who withhold themselves from that universal deal (we call them "psychotics") tends to support this view, but the issue is one of those absolutely basic phenomenological questions (called "ontological" in Chapter 10) that must for now remain in question. Even so, it is clear at this point how apparently obscure ontological issues make a whale of a difference in very vivid psychological questions, like the nature of psychosis, of interpersonal relations, and so on.

CHAPTER 10

[1] These negative statements—that the world is not merely subjective or merely objective—are expressions of a philosophical, indeed a metaphysical, view that is distinguished from idealism and realism respectively (see also Chapter 2, note 7). Both these historically salient metaphysical positions lead to contradictions and finally to misunderstandings in philosophy and especially in psychology. Phenomenology is not the only philosophy that tries to steer a course between idealism and realism, but it is the most recent and is the one that has developed alongside modern psychology. It has, for this reason, taken more from and offered more to modern psychology than have other metaphysical philosophies. Some philosophies, of course, like logical positivism are equally recent and have a lot to do with psychology, but they explicitly try to avoid metaphysics. Whether or not such avoidance is possible is a subject of extended philosophical debate, which sometimes constitutes the latent content of arguments between psychologists, as in T. W. Wann (1964).

[2] As psychologists, we are less interested in this question and in other issues about the universality of experience than we are in variations. The changes in my daughter's experience capture our attention more than the sameness. We are more interested in how people are different from one another than in how they are alike. Mammoth universal questions have been traditionally studied by philosophers, and psychologists have been more willing to assume that being simply is, that things simply are, and that experience simply is—and to inquire into less speculative and more practical questions, working from this assumption.

However, variation among people or from time to time for the same person always occurs within a set of limits. The fact that every person experiences a world—that it is always already there for him, full of meaning, supplying a referential totality within which experiences make sense—this fact is not irrelevant to psychology. Furthermore, it is not merely the presence of the world for us that is universal; it always makes itself present in terms of space, time, self-identity, and other universals of human experience. The specification of these universals of human experience and how they fit together in the human enterprise of being-in-the-world is an ontological aspect of psychology.

[3] See Chapter 9, note 9.

[4] To say that the world is always already there may seem to beg the question of where it came from—not in terms of the cosmos but in terms of psychology. That is, it is apparently true that the world is not present for the fetus but that it is present for me now. Between now and when I was a fetus, the world came to be for me. How did that happen? Jean Piaget (1929, 1954) offers us the most sensitive observations of the development of consciousness in the individual, but these observations do not account for the commonality of the world, the fact that the world I live is essentially similar to the world you live. There is a common-sense notion that you and I will obviously develop to live similar worlds because there is, after all, only one "real" physical world "out there." The world of which we speak, however, and whose commonality impresses us, is not simply a collection of common objects. More important, it is also an already existing set of meanings, a referential totality within which specific referential perception and behavior are meaningful. Hence we develop psychologically in an already existing meaningful world. Development is learning that referential totality, as well as acquiring specific perceptual objects.

The always already-present nature of the world led Martin Heidegger, in his later work, into a study of language, for language carries the burden of much of our shared reference and may supply the framework for the rest. The study of language, in this sense, is not merely the comparison of different languages and how they categorize the world differently (Whorf, 1956) but also the study of language *per se* as the constituting agent in there being reference and a totality of reference (the world) at all.

[5] If I came from a different culture, where there was neither tennis nor beer, then there would be some meanings that I would not share, and I would not understand the players' behavior as I do. Most assuredly, many meanings are culturally relative. But I would know *that* this (apparently) strange behavior had meanings; I would understand *that* I did not share in those meanings. The experience of others' behavior as puzzling merely leaves me out of their culture, not out of understanding that they have a culture. I never assume that African aborigines, whose culture I do not understand, are automatons or randomly moving reeds in the wind. I understand *that* they are being-in-the-world, *what* that process of being is like, and *what* the world is like as a setting in which to be. I never lose my fundamental sense of being-in-the-world and hence never lose the *world* as that which I have in common with others, even as I recognize (and against which standard I recognize) our more superficial differences.

[6] This assumption and the ones following it in the text are directly out of the British tradition of empirical philosophy (as practiced, for example, by John Locke, George Berkeley, and David Hume). This philosophical tradition has permeated the ways in which we represent our minds to ourselves and certainly underlies most of American psychology. Phenomenology poses a direct challenge to this tradition and these assumptions, and it appeals for confirmation to experience *as experienced*, rather than to experience as we traditionally explain it to ourselves.

[7] There is a strong bias in Western thought toward locating such variation inside myself (the notion, for example, that moods are merely the experiential results of glandular variations) and assuming that the world, in its objective presence, is constant. Our concept of the world is of the world of experience and hence is neither objective nor subjective in the traditional sense. To say that "beauty is in the eye of the beholder" violates experience as it is experienced. My experience of beauty places it not in my eye or my mind but in the world. Similarly, to say that a gray and depressing day is as it is because of a change in myself also violates the experiential data, which dictate that on a gray day the world seems flat, colorless, and depressing.

This "subjectivistic" bias of Western thought is so strong that it may indeed be difficult for us to return to experience and appreciate it as it is. But the experiential fact is that the world changes in moods. To create a psychology of moods on the basis of this experiential fact certainly flies in the face of our traditional way of thinking about mind and body. Instead of bodily events causing mental ones (the usual format), phenomenologically we would say that body also expresses our change of world; body and mind, we must remember, are abstractions from the original datum of being-in-the-world.

CHAPTER 11

[1] There is a significant complication in "establishing a language" without "doing violence to the data of lived experience." When there is already a language for the data of lived experience, establishment of *new* language would necessarily do violence. This issue is significant for the language of all social science; the later Martin Heidegger seems to have been one of the few scholars, perhaps along with Ludwig Wittgenstein, who take *natural* language as ontologically foundational.

[2] See Chapter 2, note 1, for further clarification of the relation of phenomenological psychology to other psychologies. Also see the appendix to this book.

[3] Three common features immediately stand out. First, the Skinnerian emphasis upon the environmental control of behavior, especially the

contemporaneous environment (to distinguish Skinner's thinking from "environmentalism" in general like that of John Watson), like the phenomenological starting point of being-in-the-world, places the person squarely *in the situation*, not really separable from his immediate setting if we want to understand him. Second, the Skinnerian tendency to study one organism at a time, assuming that something central to that organism's being-as-it-is may be discerned, like phenomenology's assumption that examining one's own experience is important, eschews the excessively inductive theory of truth that leads so many psychologists to compute averages and seek statistical results. Third, the Skinnerian assumption that behavior is "emitted" rather than merely provoked, like the emphasis of phenomenology on intentionality, attributes initiative and activity, rather than inertness and passivity, to the organism.

Each of these three points also highlights important differences in language and style between the two psychologies, and the complex theoretical and historical nature of these issues themselves demands a thorough analysis that we cannot give here.

[4] For a lucid description of the personology of Gordon Allport, Abraham Maslow, and H. A. Murray, see S. R. Maddi and P. T. Costa (1972). See the appendix of this book for a somewhat different slant on this topic.

[5] Carl Rogers (1973) has suggested that we keep open the possibility of other "realities" besides the one that is ordinarily reckoned in our modern, well-programmed, conscious experience. He points to extraordinary paranormal experiences, especially those of Carlos Casteneda (1971), as evidence that we ought not to be so rigid about our preconceptions of reality. I think that this plea, noble as it is, should be refined and restated in two senses. First, I do not think that we need to go to such paranormal experiences as those of Casteneda in order to find mysteries that can excite us. I know of no psychology to date that has packaged the simplest phenomenon of human perception in an adequate explanation. No matter how sophisticated we become about the mechanics of perceptual organs and the brain, we have not approached the amazing fact that there *is* experience, rather than simply mechanical interaction of things. Second, the "other realities" that are presumably glimpsed under special circumstances of drugs and religious ecstasy are not really that different from everyday experience, if only we could pay attention to experience as it is experienced instead of always understanding it in terms of our rational-functional, Newtonian frame of reference. The Newtonian world is certainly not the world of our experience; it never was. We have merely convinced ourselves that reality is as our models have said it must be, though ordinary experience contradicts it every day.

[6] For a view of the knotty moral problems confronting psychology today, see Keen (1972).

REFERENCES

Abelson, R. P., Aronson, E., McGuire, W. J., Newcomb, T. M., Rosenberg, M. J., & Tannenbaum, P. (Eds.) *Theories of cognitive consistency: A sourcebook.* Chicago: Rand McNally, 1968.

Alapack, R. J. The physiognomy of the Mueller-Lyer figure. *Journal of phenomenological psychology,* 1971, 2, 27–48.

Allport, G. W., & Vernon, P. E. *Studies in expressive movement.* New York: The Macmillan Company, 1933.

American Psychological Association. *Casebook on ethical standards of psychologists.* Washington, D.C.: American Psychological Association, 1967.

Anderson, M. *From curiosity to satiety: The American reaction to Freud in the 1920's.* Unpublished senior honors thesis, Bucknell University, 1967.

Asch, S. E. Effects of group pressure upon the modification and distortion of judgments. In E. E. Maccoby, T. M. Newcomb, & E. L. Hartley. (Eds.) *Readings in social psychology.* (3rd ed.) New York: Holt, Rinehart and Winston, 1958.

Bandura, A. *Principles of behavior modification.* New York: Holt, Rinehart and Winston, 1969.

Barton, A. *Three worlds of therapy: Freud, Jung, and Rogers.* Palo Alto: National Press Books, 1974.

Berne, E. *Games people play.* New York: Grove Press, 1964.

Beshai, J. A. Psychology's dilemma: To explain or to understand. *Journal of phenomenological psychology,* 1971 1, 209–224.

Binswanger, L. *Grundformen und Erkenntnis menschlichen Daseins.* Zurich: Neihans, 1953.

Binswanger, L. The existential analysis school of thought. In R. May, E. Angel, & H. Ellenberger. (Eds.) *Existence: A new dimension in psychology and psychiatry.* New York: Basic Books, 1958a.

Binswanger, L. The case of Ellen West. In R. May, E. Angel, & H. Ellenberger. (Eds.) *Existence: A new dimension in psychology and psychiatry.* New York: Basic Books, 1958b.

Binswanger, L. *Being-in-the-world.* (Trans. and ed. by Jacob Needleman.) New York: Basic Books, 1963.

Boring, E. G. *A history of experimental psychology.* New York: Appleton-Century-Crofts, 1950.

Boss, M. *The analysis of dreams.* New York: Philosophical Library, 1958.

Boss, M. *Psychoanalysis and daseinsanalysis.* New York: Basic Books, 1963.

Boszormenyi-Nagy, I., & Framo, J. L. (Eds.) *Intensive family therapy.* New York: Harper & Row, 1965.

Braginski, B. M., Braginski, D. D., & Ring, K. *Methods of madness: The hospital as a last resort.* New York: Holt, Rinehart and Winston, 1969.

Brentano, F. *Psychologie vom empirischen Standpunkt.* Leipzig: Duncker & Humbolt, 1874.

Buber, M. Guilt and guilt feelings. *Psychiatry,* 1957, *20,* 114-130.

Buber, M. *I and thou.* New York: Charles Scribner's Sons, 1958.

Bugental, J. F. T. *The search for authenticity.* New York: Holt, Rinehart and Winston, 1965.

Burton, A. *Modern humanistic psychotherapy.* San Francisco: Jossey-Bass, 1967.

Buytendijk, F. J. J. *Pain.* (Trans. by Eda O'Shiel.) Chicago: University of Chicago Press, 1962.

Casteneda, C. *A separate reality: Further conversations with Don Juan.* New York: Simon & Schuster, 1971.

Cloonan, T. F. Experiential and behavioral aspects of decision-making. In A. Giorgi, R. Von Eckartsberg, & W. Fischer. (Eds.) *Duquesne studies in phenomenological psychology.* Vol. 1. Pittsburgh: Duquesne University Press, 1971. Pp. 112-131.

Colaizzi, P. R. *Reflection and research in psychology.* Dubuque, Iowa: Kendall/Hunt Publishing Company, 1973.

Coles, R. *Children in crisis.* (3 vols.) Boston: Little, Brown, 1967-1971.

Coles, R. *Migrants, sharecroppers, mountaineers.* Boston: Little, Brown, 1971.

Deutsch, F., & Murphy, W. F. *The clinical interview.* New York: International Universities Press, 1955.

Eisenstein, V. W. (Ed.) *Neurotic interaction in marriage.* New York: Basic Books, 1956.

Esterson, A. *The leaves of spring.* Harmondsworth, Middlesex, England: Penguin Books, Ltd., 1972.

Ferber, A., Mendelsohn, M., & Napier, A. (Eds.) *The book of family therapy.* New York: Science House, 1972.

Festinger, L. *A theory of cognitive dissonance.* Stanford: Stanford University Press, 1957.

Festinger, L., Riecken, H. W., & Schachter, S. *When prophecy fails.* Minneapolis: University of Minnesota Press, 1956.

Fingarette, H. *The self in transformation.* New York: Basic Books, 1963.

Fischer, C. T. The testee as co-evaluator. *Journal of counseling psychology,* 1970, *17,* 70-76.

Fischer, C. T. Toward the structure of privacy: Implications for psychological assessment. In A. Giorgi, W. Fischer, & R. Von Eckartsberg. (Eds.) *Duquesne studies in phenomenological psychology.* Vol. 1. Pittsburgh: Duquesne University Press, 1971. Pp. 149-163.

Fischer, W. The faces of anxiety. *Journal of phenomenological psychology,* 1970, *1,* 21-50.

Fischer, W. The problem of unconscious motivation. In A. Giorgi, R. Von Eckartsberg, & W. Fischer. (Eds.) *Duquesne studies in phenomenological psychology.* Vol. 1. Pittsburgh: Duquesne University Press, 1971, Pp. 247-258.

Flavell, J. H. *The developmental psychology of Jean Piaget.* New York: Van Nostrand, 1963.

Foucault, M. *The order of things.* New York: Vintage, 1970.

Frankel, S. Situational determinants of three empirical principles of interpersonal attraction. Unpublished senior thesis, University of Massachusetts, 1973.

Freud, S. *Civilization and its discontents.* New York: Norton, 1961.

From, F. *Perception of other people.* New York: Columbia University Press, 1971.

Gelb, A., & Goldstein, K. Zeigen und Greifen. *Nervenarzt,* 1931.

Gendlin, E. T. *Experiencing and the creation of meaning.* New York: Free Press, 1962.

Giorgi, A. Phenomenology and experimental psychology, II. *Review of existential psychology and psychiatry,* 1966, *6,* 37-50.

Giorgi, A. *Psychology as a human science: A phenomenologically based approach.* New York: Harper & Row, 1970a.

Giorgi, A. Toward phenomenologically based research in psychology. *Journal of phenomenological psychology,* 1970b, *1,* 75-98.

Giorgi, A., Fischer, W., & Von Eckartsberg, R. (Eds.) *Duquesne studies in phenomenological psychology.* Vol. 1. Pittsburgh: Duquesne University Press, 1971.

Goffman, E. *The presentation of self in everyday life.* New York: Doubleday Anchor, 1959.

Goffman, E. *Asylums: Essays on the social situation of mental patients and other inmates.* New York: Doubleday, 1961.

Goffman, E. *Relations in public.* New York: Harper & Row, 1971.

Goldstein, L. J. Logic of explanation in Malinowskian anthropology. *Philosophy of science,* 1947, *24,* 155–166.

Grings, W. W. Cognitive factors in electrodermal conditioning. *Psychological bulletin,* 1973, *79,* 200–210.

Group for the Advancement of Psychiatry, Committee on the Family. *Treatment of families in conflict.* New York: Science House, 1970.

Haigh, G. Existential guilt: Neurotic and real. *Review of existential psychology and psychiatry,* 1961, *1,* 120–131.

Harris, T. A. *I'm okay—you're okay.* New York: Harper & Row, 1967.

Heidbreder, E. *Seven psychologies.* New York: Appleton-Century-Crofts, 1933.

Heidegger, M. *Being and time.* New York: Harper & Row, 1962.

Heider, F. *The psychology of interpersonal relations.* New York: Wiley, 1956.

Henry, J. *Pathways to madness.* New York: Random House, 1971.

Hofstadter, R. *Social Darwinism in American thought.* Philadelphia: University of Pennsylvania Press, 1944.

Horney, K. *Neurosis and human growth.* New York: Norton, 1950.

Howells, J. G. *Theory and practice of family psychotherapy.* New York: Brunner/Mazel, 1971.

Hull, C. L. *A. behavior system.* New Haven: Yale University Press, 1952.

Husserl, E. *Ideas.* London: Allen & Unwin, 1958.

Husserl, E. *Cartesian meditations.* The Hague: Nijhoff, 1960.

Husserl, E. *The idea of phenomenology.* The Hague: Nijhoff, 1968.

Husserl, E. *The crisis of the European sciences and transcendental phenomenology.* Evanston: Northwestern University Press, 1970.

James, M., & Jongeward, D. *Born to win.* Reading, Mass.: Addison-Wesley, 1971.

James, W. *Principles of psychology.* (2 vols.) New York: Holt, Rinehart and Winston, 1890.

Jones, E. E., Kanouse, D. E., Kelly, H. H., Nisbett, R. E., Valins, S., & Weiner, B. *Attribution: Perceiving the causes of behavior.* Morristown, N.J.: General Learning Press, 1972.

Jourard, S. *The transparent self: Self-disclosure and well-being.* New York: Van Nostrand, 1964.

Jourard, S. *Self-disclosure.* New York: Wiley-Interscience, 1971.

Kardiner, A., & Preble, E. *They studied man.* New York: The World Publishing Company, 1961.

Keen, E. Scheler's view of repentance and rebirth and its relevance to psychotherapy. *Review of existential psychology and psychiatry*, 1966, *6*, 84–88.

Keen, E. *Three faces of being: Toward an existential clinical psychology*. New York: Appleton-Century-Crofts, 1970.

Keen, E. *Psychology and the new consciousness*. Monterey: Brooks/Cole, 1972.

Kelly, G. *The psychology of personal constructs*. New York: Norton, 1955.

Kockelmans, J. J. Phenomenological psychology in the United States: A critical analysis of the actual situation. *Journal of phenomenological psychology*, 1971, *2*, 139–172.

Koffka, K. *Principles of Gestalt psychology*. New York: Harcourt Brace Jovanovich, 1935.

Köhler, W. *The mentality of apes*. New York: Liveright, 1925.

Köhler, W. *Dynamics in psychology*. New York: Grove Press, 1940.

Köhler, W. *Gestalt psychology*. New York: Liveright, 1947.

Kuenzli, A. E. (Ed.) *The phenomenological problem*. New York: Harper & Row, 1959.

Kuhn, T. S. *The structure of scientific revolutions*. Chicago: University of Chicago Press, 1962.

Kwant, R. C. *Phenomenology of social existence*. Pittsburgh: Duquesne University Press, 1965.

Laing, R. D. *The politics of experience*. New York: Pantheon, 1967.

Laing, R. D. *Self and others*. New York: Pantheon, 1969.

Laing, R. D., & Esterson, A. *Sanity, madness, and the family*. Harmondsworth, Middlesex, England: Penguin Books Ltd., 1970.

Lapointe, F. H. Phenomenology, psychoanalysis, and the unconscious. *Journal of phenomenological psychology*, 1971, *2*, 5–26.

Lauffer, M. A phenomenological study of empathy. Unpublished master's thesis, Bucknell University, 1971.

Levi, B. Critique of Piaget's theory of intelligence: A phenomenological approach. *Journal of phenomenological psychology*, 1972, *3*, 99–112.

Lewin, K. *A dynamic theory of personality*. New York: McGraw-Hill, 1935.

Lewin, K. *Principles of topological psychology*. New York: McGraw-Hill, 1936.

Lidz, T., Fleck, S., & Cornelison, A. *Schizophrenia and the family*. New York: International Universities Press, 1965.

Lynd, H. M. *On shame and the search for identity*. New York: Science Editing, 1961.

Lyons, J. A bibliographic introduction to phenomenology and existentialism. In R. May (Ed.) *Existential psychology*. New York: Random House, 1961. Pp. 101–126.

Lyons, J. *Psychology and the measure of man.* New York: Free Press, 1963.

Lyons, J. The hidden dialogue in experimental research. *Journal of phenomenological psychology,* 1970, *1,* 19–30.

Maddi, S. R., & P. T. Costa. *Humanism in personology.* Chicago, Aldine, 1972.

Malinowski, B. *Magic, science and religion and other essays.* New York: Free Press, 1948.

May R. *Psychology and the human dilemma.* New York: Van Nostrand, 1967.

May, R., Angle, E., & Ellenberger, H. *Existence: A new dimension in psychiatry and psychology.* New York: Basic Books, 1958.

Mead, M. *Sex and temperament in three primitive societies.* New York: Morrow, 1935.

Merleau-Ponty, M. *The phenomenology of perception.* New York: Humanities Press, 1962.

Merleau-Ponty, M. The child's relations with others. In M. Merleau-Ponty, *The primacy of perception.* Evanston: Northwestern University Press, 1964a.

Merleau-Ponty, M. *The primacy of perception.* Evanston: Northwestern University Press, 1964b.

Merleau-Ponty, M. *The structure of behavior.* Boston: Beacon Press, 1964c.

Minuchin, S., Montalvo, B., Guerney, B. G., Rosman, B. L., & Schumer, F. *Families of the slums.* New York: Basic Books, 1967.

Natanson, M. *The journeying self.* Reading, Mass.: Addison-Wesley, 1970.

Natanson, M. (Ed.) *Phenomenology and the social sciences.* Vol. 1. Evanston: Northwestern University Press, 1973.

Niell, A. S. *Summerhill.* New York: Hart, 1960.

Orne, M. On the social psychology of the psychological experiment. *American psychologist,* 1962, *17,* 776–783.

Pavenstedt, E. A comparison of the child-rearing environment of upper-lower and very low-lower class families. *American journal of orthopsychiatry,* 1965, *35,* 89–98.

Piaget, J. *The child's conception of the world.* New York: Harcourt Brace Jovanovich, 1929.

Piaget, J. *The construction of reality in the child.* New York: Basic Books, 1954.

Piaget, J. *Insights and illusions of philosophy.* New York: The World Publishing Company, 1971.

Radnitzky, G. *Contemporary schools of metascience.* New York: Humanities Press, 1970.

Ricoeur, P. *The symbolism of evil.* New York: Harper & Row, 1967.

Ricoeur, P. *Freud and philosophy.* New Haven: Yale University Press, 1970.

Rieff, P. *Freud: The mind of the moralist.* New York: The Viking Press, 1959.

Rogers, C. *Counseling and psychotherapy.* Boston: Houghton Mifflin, 1942.

Rogers, C. *Client-centered therapy.* Boston: Houghton Mifflin, 1951.

Rogers, C. *On becoming a person.* Boston: Houghton Mifflin, 1961.

Rogers, C. Some new challenges. *American psychologist,* 1973, *28,* 379–387.

Rosenthal, R. *Experimenter effects in behavioral research.* New York: Appleton-Century-Crofts, 1966.

Rotter, J. B. Generalized expectancies for internal versus external control of reinforcement. *Psychological monographs,* 1966, *80,* No. 1 (Whole No: 609).

Sartre, J.-P. *Being and nothingness.* New York: Philosophical Library, 1956.

Sartre, J.-P. *Nausea.* New York: New Directions, 1959.

Scheler, M. *The nature of sympathy.* New Haven: Yale University Press, 1954.

Schütz, A. *The phenomenology of the social world.* Evanston: Northwestern University Press, 1967.

Schütz, A. *On phenomenology and social relations.* Chicago: University of Chicago Press, 1970.

Skinner, B. F. *Science and human behavior.* New York: The Macmillan Company, 1953.

Skinner, B. F. *Beyond freedom and dignity.* New York: Alfred A. Knopf, 1972.

Snygg, D., and Combs, A. W. *Individual behavior.* New York: Harper & Row, 1949.

Spiegelberg, H. *The phenomenological movement.* (2 vols.) The Hague: Nijhoff, 1960.

Spiegelberg, H. *Phenomenology in psychology and psychiatry.* Evanston: Northwestern University Press, 1972.

Stevick, E. L. An empirical investigation of the experience of anger. In A. Giorgi, W. Fischer, & R. Von Eckartsberg. (Eds.) *Duquesne studies in phenomenological psychology.* Vol. 1. Pittsburgh: Duquesne University Press, 1971. Pp. 132–148.

Strasser, S. *Phenomenology and the human sciences.* Pittsburgh: Duquesne University Press, 1963.

Straus, E. *The primary world of the senses.* New York: Free Press, 1963.

Straus, E. (Ed.) *Phenomenology: Pure and applied.* Pittsburgh: Duquesne University Press, 1964.

Straus, E. *Phenomenological psychology.* New York: Basic Books, 1966.

Szasz, T. S. *The manufacture of madness.* New York: Harper & Row, 1970.

Titchener, E. B. *Systematic psychology: Prolegomena.* Ithaca: Cornell University Press, 1966.

Tolman, E. C. *Behavior and psychological man.* Berkeley: University of California Press, 1966.

Underwood, B. J. The representativeness of rote verbal learning. In A. W. Melton. (Ed.) *Categories of human learning.* New York: Academic Press, 1964.

Van den Berg, J. H. *A different existence.* Pittsburgh: Duquesne University Press, 1973.

Van der Post, L. *The dark eye of Africa.* New York: Morrow, 1955.

Von Eckartsberg, R. An approach to experiential social psychology. In A. Giorgi, W. Fischer, and R. Von Eckartsberg. (Eds.) *Duquesne studies in phenomenological psychology.* Vol. 1. Pittsburgh: Duquesne University Press, 1971. Pp. 325–372.

Wann, T. W. *Behaviorism and phenomenology.* Chicago: University of Chicago Press, 1964.

Watson, J. *Behaviorism.* Chicago: University of Chicago Press, 1924.

Whorf, B. L. *Language, thought and reality.* New York: Wiley, 1956.

Whyte, W. F. *Street corner society: The social structure of an Italian slum.* Chicago: University of Chicago Press, 1943.

Zaner, R. M. *The way of phenomenology.* New York: Pegasus, 1970.

Zuk, G. H. *Family therapy: A triadic-based approach.* New York: Behavioral Publications, 1971.

NAME INDEX

SUBJECT INDEX

Made in the USA
San Bernardino, CA
06 January 2016